New Horizons Beckon

by

Patricia Coates

Horseshoe Publications, Warrington, Cheshire

ISBN 1 899310 23 1

British Library Cataloguing in Publication Data
A Catalogue Record for this book is available from the British Library

First Published in 1999 by
Horseshoe Publications
Box 37, Kingsley, Warrington
Cheshire WH6 8DR

Printed and bound in Great Britain by
Print Express Services Ltd.
Frodsham, Cheshire

Preface

Hearth and home is fortress and castle
Of all Englishmen, legend has said,
While to labour at desk, screen and factory,
Is the mainstay of life, where we're led

Far be it from me to deny this,
The freedom of bondage is known,
Security matters, not choices,
Man's a fool who can give up his home.

But what of the one who is curious,
Not content with the treadmill's demands.
Here a road, there a hill, new horizons
Beckon onwards and out to new lands

Dedication

To Eric – the driving force in the enterprise – and Robert, Edmund, Richard and Nicholas, our forbearing sons.

Chapter One

Wind of Change

'Comes over one an absolute necessity to move'
D H Lawrence Sea & Sardinia.

The journey was not undertaken on foot, or bicycle, nor did we travel on a donkey, and as for hot-air balloons or bi-planes, well such flights of fancy were out of our sphere. This is merely a tale of two slightly mad middle-aged folk who took it into their heads to wander around Europe in a diminutive two-seater sports car. We loved our elderly lean, green, Lancia Fulvia and believed her capable of anything, including Alpine crossings loaded to the gunwales with a ludicrous amount of luggage. Our needs were as unpredictable as destination or distance in this extemporaneous escapade, but the Lancia gave a good account of herself coping well with the excessive demands.

It all began one morning in July 1982. To all outward appearances it was an ordinary departure, an arrival at the pierhead with the customary hour to spare before sailing, but for us this was an extraordinary ferry crossing. It was to be an end and a beginning, the closing of a whole chapter of our lives and a precarious new start.

It was precarious in more ways than one; inexperience, underfunding, and then at this the eleventh hour, there was the threat of a seamen's strike. The morning's sailing of the Manx Viking from Douglas, Isle of Man to Heysham hung in the balance. The one-hour loading time went by and nothing happened. Drivers left their cars and wandered back and forth trying to discover the reason for the delay, not in this instance being able to attribute it to adverse weather conditions.

Eventually word travelled along the waiting line of cars, a seamen's meeting had been convened to discuss the possibility of coming out in support of trouble at the port of Harwich.

Our hearts sank. This was no way to begin a journey of magnitude, into the unknown as it were, baulked on our own doors-step yet without a door to return to. Having metamorphosed from sedate middle-aged citizens into intrepid explorers newly hatched from the chrysalis of conformity it was unfitting to have those symbolic bridges blown sky-high before leaving home shores. What ignominy!

It took two hours, two tense nerve-stretching hours for a verdict to be reached and the news broke that a strike was averted. Indefinite delay would have jeopardised the second leg of the journey, a crucial one of only two sailings per week from Newcastle to Oslo. However, conjecture about possible alternatives was fortunately unnecessary and we breathed freely again as the Manx Viking slipped her moorings. And as the shores of the island receded merging with the all-pervasive backdrop of grey sky we had time to meditate on the various phases of life. This was goodbye to a valuable period that could never be reclaimed but for all that, future prospects predominated in our thoughts allowing no regrets.

This consequential day was the culmination of half a year's preparation following several months when the idea was merely in embryo. In the summer of 1981 the first step towards the ultimate freedom of motorised drifting came with a holiday drive to Italy. The quiet hills of Emilia Romagna had whetted our appetite to explore more of Europe's less publicised corners and if this could be achieved out of season, so much the better.

So the virus took hold and slowly developed, incubated no doubt during the long dark months of winter. There was an added factor deserving of some consideration when attempting to explain what friends and family looked upon as an acute case of irresponsibility and that was an end to my role as the grand matriarch. Four sons had, one by one, reached the age of discretion and I was not longer indispensable, a shock to the system after thirty years of total commitment.

When things came to a head and the momentous decision was fact it was time to consider ways and means. First of all came the review of assets. These would have seemed ludicrously inadequate to most people of normal intelligence but we refused to accept this as a stumbling block. The family house was surplus to requirements. The rooms once sheltering six bodies echoed with the ghosts of former times and mocked my demotion to housekeeper. We rattled about like the proverbial peas in a pod and the fact that it could be converted to capital was welcomed with unequivocal confidence. Likewise the furniture, furnishings a collection of books, ornaments and pictures, the sale of which would bring only a fleeting pang. A few of the most treasured items were to be retained and stored, so maintaining the nucleus of a Coates home as a sort of insurance policy against disaster.

This shedding of the accumulations of a lifetime appalled the inveterate hoarders amongst our friends. 'We admire your courage' some said, which roughly translated meant 'You must be crazy'. Others did not scruple to disguise their disapproval. Lack of security and serious underfunding were amongst the not unreasonable criticisms levelled against our project, 'and what of inflation' they cried, but we remained impervious. The disease that had us in its grip was deaf to words like inflation, it just had to run its course and reach a crisis before any amelioration could come about.

A question voiced more that once, both before and during our voluntary retirement and subsequent travels was how we would fill our days. It seemed beyond comprehension that one should no longer be part of the work-orientated routine before illness or old age forced the situation upon one. Robert Louis Stephenson had this kind of question summed up in his observation that 'Such people lack curiosity and would pine for their desks if set aboard ship, or brought into the country'. Curiosity, that is the emotion that drives the traveller from the comfort and security of his own four walls into, what? We had no way of knowing, but the threat of straitened circumstances, discomfort, loneliness could not undermine our curiosity or the longing for new experience.

It was remarkable how quickly events carried us along once the wheels were set in motion. 'Cronk Beg' the erstwhile Coates residence was sold within a week of advertising, and although we were naturally pleased, the elation was tempered by the merest hint of apprehension as all was signed, sealed, and delivered. Well, we are in it now up to the neck, I thought; there can be no turning back now. As it was, the weeks that followed left scant time for either dreams or regrets as the house filled with bargain hunters. Gradually all our furniture and trappings disappeared and it was time for us to find a stopgap. Eric had still a term's notice to complete at Ballakermeen High School, from Easter to mid-July so we experienced the first of what was to become our natural mode of shelter, the furnished flat.

I should introduce here the mundane but necessary hard fact of life, the proposed financial arrangement for the coming trip. We were in luck so far as interest rates were concerned. They were an extremely favourable 14% for fixed period investment, and every penny we could raise we tied up for three years which gave us a tidy assured income. This went some way to solving the security problem but of course we were still dangerously close to the edge of the slippery slope in some people's eyes. This did not worry me unduly, most of my life had been spent making ends meet for the family of six on one income so my dreams of adventure were not to be baulked for the lack of a little luxury.

That final term was the most trying of all the months of preparation. After the disposal of home and belongings there was nothing productive to be done until the last minute. Social life had an undercurrent of sadness coloured by impending leave-taking. Part of us seemed to have already left and conversations were stilted and repetitive as though fixed in this time and this place. It was an odd sensation.

The breathing space had its beneficial side. It gave time to brush up on languages, school French and night-class Italian. We pored avidly over maps by the hour and read a great deal. And what did we read? Travel of course, anything and everything we could lay our hands on relating to journeys past and present, from Goethe to D H Lawrence all over the place. Hilaire Belloc walking to Rome and Laurie Lee across Spain, R.L.S. getting along on a donkey and, not to be outdone; Penelope Chetwold with her Spanish pony. 'Two Middle-aged Ladies in Andalucia' I even re-read that timeless spirit-lifter of the intrepid Jerome K Jerome and his fellows cycling on the Bummel. No one could have accused us of not being well tutored in the art, or the theory at least, of moving from A to B.

I itched with anticipation, felt saturated with scents of almond and mimosa, had visions of hillsides rippling with silvery olives. Oh it was all heady stuff but my feet were not allowed to rise too far from the ground. Early in May, there occurred an unusual outbreak of flu and for the first time in my life, I succumbed. I went down like a pricked balloon and was tied to my bed for a week. This was followed by a recurrence of an old complaint, a nasty attack of sciatica and anyone who is familiar with this adversity will know that prolonged sitting is sheer hell. This had me worried I must confess, for travels in a Lancia could hardly be accomplished standing.

All these trials and tribulations passed, and with unswerving inevitability time passed too. The Lancia and Eric and myself were at last primed and ready to go, the Lancia a little top heavy perhaps but at this stage, what to take and what to leave behind was still a critical question. With experience, we learned to be a little more circumspect. And here we were with the crisis of embarkation behind us and leisure to muse on the immediate future. To begin with the journey was programmed to break us in gently as it were. Robert, our eldest son, had been living and working in Norway for the past year and this was an ideal opportunity to visit him in his adopted country. He was the organist and musical co-ordinator of the small town of Vestnes in fjord country of western Norway which was some 300 miles by road from either Oslo or Bergen. Our route was to be via the former and although ultimately our hearts and minds yearned for the south, for the cities and equable climate of the Mediterranean there was no hurry. Pressures of time no longer affected us and meanwhile there was Robert and his fjords and mountains to entice and a whole new way of life to explore. The magnitude of what lay within our grasp was almost unbelievable.

Chapter Two

Land of the Mountain King

'What's a man's first duty?
The answers brief. - 'to be himself'.   *Ibsen.*

The second embarkation passed without incident and we found ourselves aboard a rather grander vessel that the little Manx workhorse that ferried us over the Irish Sea. At 10.00 am on July 27th the D.S.D.F. ferry ENGLAND left North Shields at the start of a scheduled 28-hour voyage to Oslo. She negotiated the river in the care of the pilot until we reached Tynemouth and the open sea and then she was on her own.

The day was gloomy and overcast with a blustery wind that filled the queasy traveller with misgivings, making him wonder what the devil made him decide to leave his own shores. The 'blow' gathered strength making reading and even talking uncomfortable, and so the day dragged on. The ship's well-appointed lounges and restaurants took on the ambience of a Marie Celeste film set rather than that of a holiday ferry service.

We retired early to a cabin in the bowels of the ship; six or seven decks below the public rooms, but there was still no escaping the disorientating pitch and roll. I was convinced there would be no sleep, it seemed impossible with the din of crashing waves so close to our quarters, not to mention the bangs, creaks, and groans made by the very fabric of the tortured bulkhead. But I needn't have worried. The rhythmic movement worked like a charm bringing blessed unconsciousness to obliterate all sense of the storm.

The morning brought a wonderful change. The ship was as steady as a rock with only the throb of diesel engines to remind us of our whereabouts. Although it was early when we woke in the total darkness, we quickly dressed and made our way above decks, glad to leave the cell-like cabin and curious to find out where we were. It is not often that I rise with the summer sun but it was a pleasure to be outside on such a wonderfully transformed morning. The sea was not only flat calm but it streamed with light from the rising sun sitting at the end of a pathway of molten gold. Could this be the same world, the same ocean and sky that had loured so menacingly only yesterday.

Despite the early hour, we were not the only ones on deck. Others were already out enjoying the dramatic sea change and the change in behaviour was no less dramatic. From taciturn self-absorption, there emerged a gregarious bonhomie and greetings and smile were the order of the day. The morning exuded the joy of life.

From the faintly visible landmass on the port side, we assumed our position to be somewhere along Norway's southern coast, while to starboard a faint shadow on the horizon marked mainland Denmark. This must be the Skagerrak. There are words, usually place names, that in common with smells have an amazing capacity for triggering off nostalgia, and this was one of these. The name evoked another, hero of the great cinema years following the Second World War, the inimitable Danny Kaye. In one of his films he played the part of Hans Christian Anderson endearing himself to millions of fans with his droll song and dance performance: the tongue-twisting Skagerrak-Kattegat lyric. It was a showstopper of the period.

By mid-day the England was inside the 66 mile long Oslo fjord, a quite remarkable channel that is littered with islets, some so close that you felt almost able to reach out and touch them and some so small there was scarcely space for one timber holiday hut. Almost all Norwegian families have a retreat, a hytte, either by water for sailing enthusiasts or in the mountains for skiing, trekking or climbing. Sport and the great outdoors are of prime importance in their lives, work being a poor runner-up, a necessary evil endured in order to keep the wolf from the door and finance leisure activities. One could say that this is a healthy application of priorities.

The ship steered unerringly through the obstacle course of islands giving her passengers an entertaining mini-fjord cruise. The approach to Oslo must be amongst the most beautiful seaways in the world. There was diversion aboard too with a spontaneous concert on the sunlit promenade deck. The musicians were a group of students carrying a variety of string and woodwind instruments which they put to good use, the impromptu show was very much appreciated. Music like food seems to take on an extra dimension when served 'al fresco'.

The reference to food reminds me that this was indeed rather special. The standard of catering on board the England was excellent and with the improvement in weather conditions on the second day we were able to do it full justice. Seafoods, fresh or smoked salmon and king-sized prawns in particular, were exceptional. Maybe it was simply a case of heightened awareness fuelled by excitement, but whatever the cause the memory of pure enjoyment of food has rarely since been equalled.

It was almost 3 o'clock when we slid gently alongside and tied up. We had a few anxious moments as we waited for the Lancia to be crane-lifted ashore. She was one of a dozen or so cars to travel on open deck, the car decks being full to capacity. It was an unnerving experience to watch the diminutive vehicle and all our worldly goods hovering high above the quayside until her wheels were in contact with terra-firma, ready to carry us on to the next stage of the journey. Three hundred miles of unfamiliar roads lay ahead so there was no time to loiter on this occasion in Norway's intriguing capitol. Making a mental note to drive on the right, we drove out of the terminal anxiously watching for route E.6. while negotiating the busy harbour-side traffic.

Strange cities can often present problems when tackling outward routes. It is easy enough to follow city centre signs on the way in but the reverse is not always so straight-forward. It is especially frustrating when the crucial sign is obscured by another vehicle, or even overgrown foliage, which happens not infrequently. It might be glimpsed out of the corner of your eye at the most significant junction as you sail past in a tidal wave of traffic, in the wrong lane naturally. In such circumstances the most confident navigator might be driven to the indignity of having to ask the way, a terrible blow to ones self respect, but fortunately my navigational pride was not put to the test on this occasion, the E.6. fell in our way without the least effort on my part.

The first hurdle behind us, we had now to be cautious of another pit-fall, the risk of exceeding speed limits, which in Norway are rigorously adhered to. The law is strict with instant penalties for overstepping the mark, heavy fines payable on the spot for speeding and in the case of driving under the influence of alcohol the sentence is automatically imprisonment. There is I am told a waiting list for this period of atonement but no getting out of it. Although the law may sound implacable it seems to work reasonably well with the majority acting accordingly with an even flow of traffic and a minimal number of queue jumpers. It seemed a little slow at first but when we adjusted it was infinitely kinder to the nervous system.

The E.6. was a well maintained trunk road, there are no motorways as such in Norway, and even this major route in and out of the capitol carried only a moderate amount of traffic. It was the motorist's dream and consequently progress northwards was invariably smooth. The route took us along the rich farming valley of Gudbrandsdal, closely hugging the shores of Norway's longest lake Mjøsa, to Dombàs a major crossroads where we changed direction for the western fjords. There is a saying that Dombàs is the draughtiest place in Norway with chill winds attacking it from every compass point but this day proved to be the exception. It was hot, incredibly hot, not at all, what we had expected of Scandinavia, and as the miles, or rather kilometres ticked by, we received the first intimations of dehydration. This condition can be said to be an occupational hazard of distance motoring in hot climates but we had not given a thought to the possibility on the journey north. The temptation to keep going when the going is as easy as this seemed is strong, but in my role of co-driver, I managed to convince the man at the wheel that a break was desirable and necessary. Out came the new camping gaz stove, an invaluable piece of equipment that was to revitalise us on many occasions in the weeks to come, and within minutes that sine qua non of the Englishman, a good cup of tea, was setting us up for the final leg of the journey.

After Dombàs there was a marked change in the landscape. The road led into a region of mountains following a turbulent river that crossed and re-crossed our path in wide meanders. At first the valley was wide and green, the mountains softly wooded but gradually they closed in, menacing, sombre. We were now hemmed in by the racing river and sheer rock-sided gorge. Few trees could find a hold on the steep sided cliffs but there were plenty of waterfalls, falling from the heights to the green river, they hung like gleaming silvery-white streamers. This was troll-country. The harsh light and long shadows deceived the eye creating fantastic affects on the rock face. Weird outcrops took the form of ugly long-nosed giants, troll-like and undoubtedly malevolent. It was easy to understand how this dour landscape produced such an apposite folklore.

Quite suddenly the gorge opened up and we were in Àndalsnes an important fjord-side railway junction. From here, the road followed the great in-bites of the fjords, through villages, through dark tunnels that telescoped the road into dazzling points of low sunlight. Through Vikebukt, round the Tresfjord valley and finally, as darkness fell we reached our destination, Vestnes.

The details of the reunion come back to me as a confusion of pain and joy, utter tiredness, incoherent talk all suffused with a bland happiness. Robert produced omelettes, bread and butter and tea, the most we were capable of dealing with, and then, aware of our fatigue, he led us to our lodgings. His own bachelor apartment would not accommodate us

11

but Bredeli, the minister of the church of which Robert was the organist had stepped into the breach. We were to sleep in the Prestegard; a large white-painted timber house built in the late 19th century.

The first memory I have of the priest's house is waking to the fresh smell of polished pine. I opened my eyes and oriented myself to see a sparsely furnished room containing two pine box-beds; surprisingly comfortable with well sprung mattresses and white cotton duvets. The polished wood floor was bare but for a couple of woven bedside mats and similar but smaller woven hangings decorated the pine walls. A chest of drawers and chair in the same mellow wood completed the furnishings. I pulled aside the brightly coloured cotton curtains to take a look at the outside world in daylight but to my surprise, there was nothing to be seen. A thick white mist concealed everything to within a few feet of the house, making it impossible to visualise the neighbouring geography, the high mountain ranges and extensive waterways described often and enthusiastically by our immigrant son. Where were they in relation to our window? – when would they reappear? It was very frustrating.

On the way out of the house to join Robert for breakfast, we ran into our host, the priest Bredeli who together with his son was about to leave for a fishing trip. The boy of about twelve years solemnly shook hands and introduced himself as Arne, a practice that we found unusual on this the first day in a foreign land but it was one to which we soon became accustomed. People do not wait for a third person to introduce them, they do it themselves clearly giving their names. It seemed to make for easier identification when there are many new faces and names to learn. Bredeli assured us that the mist would shortly clear away, 'There will be good weather today and then you will see our land and mountains' he said.

We took the opportunity to thank Bredeli for the use of our comfortable dormitory and to admire his splendid house but to our surprise, he seemed not to share the sentiment. He went on to explain that its size was something of a liability for modern conditions. It was designed for the days when country priests would frequently be called upon to offer hospitality to travelling clergy, perhaps the Bishop and his entire entourage. Distances between towns and adverse weather conditions could well have extended these visits indefinitely so it was imperative that suites of rooms be kept for such eventualities. One servant was fully employed in keeping the old wood-burning stoves well stoked and as there was one in every room of this rambling old house it must have been an unending round, rather like the painting of the Forth Bridge. The old stoves were no longer in use having been replaced by modern central heating but because of its extent it was not a hundred per cent efficient but yet was very expensive to operate.

It was good to exchange news with Robert over a relaxed breakfast, the conversation flowing rather more intelligibly after a good night's sleep, and plans for the week were discussed beginning with those for the day. It was a working one for Robert and as our own priority was to get to know Vestnes, we agreed to go our separate ways proposing to meet back at the flat for a meal in the evening.

The moment when the mist cleared about mid-morning was magnificent. It appeared to be all the more spectacular because of the provocative delay and when the curtain of mist did rise the scene was a coup de théàtre. Mountains with jagged saw-toothed heights, snow pockets, and wooded slopes towered above the most tranquil water imaginable. And the meadows so very green and houses so brightly painted, surrounded by neatly kept open gardens. No walls, fences or hedges divided one plot from its neighbour, simply flower beds and berry bushes. And the sun now shone with warmth and theatrical brilliance.

Vestnes is a fairly small community situated on the southern shore of the six-mile wide Romsdal fjord with a direct ferry service to Molde. It was interesting to watch the interchange of bus and ferry, the bus from Ålesund being perfectly synchronised to arrive at the terminal the moment the ferry discharged its passengers. A few moments of bustling activity was all it took for the change over and away each went leaving a deserted jetty and the ruffled water of the wake from the rapidly diminishing ferry. We were impressed by the efficiency of the interconnections between the public transport systems and also by the amazing way in which these boats could swallow a line of waiting cars, vans, and lorries with apparent ease. They rarely seemed big enough yet equally rarely did we see anyone left behind.

Luxuriously we poked around in a purposeless way and so came upon a fleet of tankers at rest in a most unlikely setting, a quiet inlet hidden from the town by a low headland. Five huge tankers parked side by side was an odd enough sight in this rural backwater but what was even more remarkable was that they were all British. This was one of those unaccountable trade lulls and these vast transport carriers had found themselves redundant, compelled to wait for a reversal in the economic situation. Each vessel was manned by a skeleton crew of enforced expatriates, some of them having been out of commission for close on two years. We wondered whether any attempt had been made to integrate with the locals and apparently, though slow to start, this was now happening. The men were receiving and accepting invitations to social functions, church services and the like which must have been an unusual state of affairs for the normally nomadic men of the sea.

After supper, Robert proposed a short drive into the hills. He took us on a saetervei, a rough mountain track whose pebbly surface was like that of a bed of marbles. These hair-raising roads are common throughout Norwegian hill country, they are less susceptible to the rigours of winter than tarmac or at least they cost less to maintain. Leaving the car in a small clearing we walked through pine and birch woods along a lovely fragrant footpath cushioned with pine needles that led to the shores of a lake. This was Frostadvatn, and like the fjord that had emerged from the morning's mist, it was incredibly mirror-smooth. The reflected surroundings were perfectly duplicated with barely a ripple to remind you that it was really water.

We sat for awhile by the water's edge talking quietly with a sort of reverence usually reserved for sacred places, it would be a violation to shatter such deep tranquillity with too deliberate or robust a voice. Reluctantly we noticed the failing light; it was getting late and time to retrace the path through the woods. Robert lead the way and suddenly without warning went off at a tangent up a rough scrub covered hillside urging us to follow in his wake. Breathless we arrived at the top to be presented with a wonderful panorama, an extensive view over Tomrefjord now ablaze with all the colour of a full-blown sunset. In the dense wood under the lee of the hill, there was no hint of the majestic vision to be seen from the top but Robert knew he had been here before. It must have been inordinately late for July days are long in this land of the mid-night sun, but the old clock-watching habit was already weakening as we abandoned ourselves to the new regimen.

Such was the measure of the days that followed. Introductions supported by invitations and hospitality quite overwhelmed us and many of these open-hearted welcoming people have since become firm friends. One of the first of many such encounters was with Per and Turid Moen who live in a delightful timber house on the wooded shores of Tomrefjord. They invited us to join them for a fishing excursion in their small boat one idyllic afternoon and although the fish refused to bite this could not detract from the pleasure. For what can be more agreeable than drifting and dreaming on calm deep-green waters under a perfect blue sky interspersed with a little desultory philosophy as the time and place demanded. Our self imposed exodus often provoked speculation, more especially at the outset when even our own prospects were vague.

Later, back at the house in the woods we were entertained to Norwegian tea. This is a fairly standard meal of open sandwiches often with the sweetish brown cheese from the Gudbrandsdal valley, the lush farming country of our route from Oslo. There are usually fish balls too, a rather bland white concoction made from their excellent cod but to us it seems a poor substitute for the original. Yul brod was more to our taste, a spicy fruit loaf that was once reserved for the Christmas season but now accompanied by bowls of summer fruits, shinning red currants and strawberries and raspberries which, though ripening later in Norway are of very good quality and flavour. The Moen's daughter, three year old Embla amused and astonished us by her capacity to consume vast quantities of ice cream without being sick. She must have enjoyed a cast-iron constitution.

Another friend turned up; the pretext for fresh pots of tea and coffee, both taken strong, black and without milk or sugar, and when all demands had been finally satisfied an impromptu soiree was devised. A few chords on the piano, then someone produced a recorder, a flute appeared and Sigmund, the late comer, remembered that he just happened to have his trombone in the boot of his car. It was a strange ensemble but a convivial one and we found ourselves, not for the first time, amazed by the average Norwegian's grasp of the English language. There were very few occasions when an interpreter was called for.

Apart from the proximity of Molde, about which I will say more later, there is also the sizeable town of Ålesund within comparatively easy reach of Vestnes. The topography of Ålesund is interesting; the main part of the town spanning three islands that form the shape of a fishhook, and the surrounding waters interspersed by dozens more. It must be one of the most photogenic and most photographed towns in all Norway, the perfect viewpoint being from Aksla, a small mountain in the very centre of the main island in the heart of the town's business centre. This bird's-eye view is a must for every visitor even though it entails a climb up the path of a thousand steps as it has been dubbed by the locals. In fact there are less than two hundred but they are steep and to the uninitiated, it feels like a thousand.

The view from a platform know as the flat iron, is well worth the effort. The multifarious islands spread themselves into the distance, their coastal waters busy with ferries, pleasure craft and fishing boats with an occasional luxury liner for good measure. Immediately below Aksla are the colourful clustering buildings of the main town while inland lies the great bulk of the snow-topped Sunnmøre range of mountains.

The town takes its name from the main intersecting channel – the Eel Sound – and it was from here early last century that the town grew. There is little to be seen of the old town as most of Ålesund's original buildings were destroyed in a great fire in January 1904 but one that survived can be seen in Kirkegata. It is an average family sized house that was once home to eight families, the total number of persons reputed to be sixty-one. This would be around the 1860's when overcrowding was rife and living space at a premium. The new town that was built after the fire is the one we see today and was designed in a distinctive art nouveau style claimed to be one of the few remaining examples of the genre.

As we were leaving Ålesund to return home, we deviated slightly to visit the ancient stone church at Borgund. It is a solid little building that gives the impression of being at one with its surroundings, a harmonious setting of stately pine trees and the ubiquitous still waters, but it was the organ not the architecture or its setting that caused our digression. The church boasted a fine instrument by Marcussen that was highly rated throughout Norway and consequently attracted regular recitalists for concert, recording, and broadcasting purposes. It was greatly coveted by Robert who never missed a chance to use it himself, and when, at a later date, the organists post became vacant his application was happily successful. However, it was the resident organist Arne Hadland who just happened to be on the point of giving one of a series of summer afternoon concerts. This caused something of a dilemma as Robert was himself due to play at an evening entertainment some distance away and time was pressing, but he decided it could be done and far be it for us to demur. Bach preludes and fugues combined with the famous Marcussen could not be denied.

We made the evening venue by the skin of our teeth – what was I saying about the obsolescent time consciousness? ah well, once away on our own things would be different. This was our first experience of a Norwegian Musikkandakt, a form of musical entertainment punctuated by short sermons delivered by lay members of the church, on this occasion Aslaug Bjermeland, a local farmer's wife. Robert played Bach, Buxtehude, Bridge and Wesley, there was some fine singing by a tenor, Rolf Haheim, and the whole was rounded off with a couple of rousing hymns by the audience. Afterwards it was time to catch up on local gossip and the little octagonal timber church resounded with conversation and hearty laughter. No concessions here to ecclesiastical establishment, the place was now their social centre. Bredeli and his wife and some of their children, I believe they had five at this time, attended the function in an unofficial capacity and while our personal mentor was otherwise engaged Bredeli stepped in to point out and explain some of Tresfjord church's whimsicalities.

It has a strangely bizarre interior, a riot of barbaric design and colour that is a sort of cross between Byzantinism and the art of the marine artificer. The carved and painted wooden rood screen and pulpit reminded me of the old figurehead carvings that once adorned ship's prows, and the story attached to the splendidly primitive altar reredos rather confirmed the connection. In this instant, the work was known to have been done by a seventeen-century craftsman who was paid three barrels of corn for his labour. He was a boat builder.

The week flew by but before turning south we had one particularly eventful and significant day, it was the day that we met our future daughter in-law without being aware of what was to come. Early on Saturday morning we took the ferry to Molde across the calm Romsdal fjord. It is a busy commercial and industrial county centre with a population of 21,000, - a popular port of call for luxury liners, and a venue for an international annual jazz festival. The town also claims the attractive signature 'The City of Roses' and thereby hangs a tale. Molde is a modern city that has grown from disaster but unlike Ålesund, whose destruction was accidental, Molde's fate was a deliberate act of war. It was systematically obliterated by bombing as retaliation for giving shelter to King Haakon and members of his government during their flight from the German invasion of 1940. All that remained were a few scattered houses but the spirit of the people withstood the holocaust as the new town itself surely testifies. One victim of the bombing that time has proved irreplaceable however was a unique crimson rose. Its particular claim to fame was an unusual heavy scent that was said to carry far on the breeze, greeting homebound ships as they sailed up the fjord. After the war, a German horticulturist attempted to propagate a replacement as a gesture of goodwill and the result of his work was presented to Molde by the citizens of the German town of Elmshorn. The rose took happily to its new environment, thriving and multiplying until today when it can be seen all over the town, but there is one significant difference. It has scarcely any scent, that it seems is lost forever.

The morning's sightseeing reached a high point, literally and figuratively, when we drove up to Varden, a vantage point above the town from where you can count 87 peaks of the Romsdal and Sunnmøre alps, a superb view even by Norway's superlative scenic standards.

It was then time to move on to catch another ferry from Hollingsholm to the offshore island of Aukra, which was the main objective of the day's outing. We were to visit the Lervik family, Gunnar and Inger and their daughter Else Marie. We had heard of the friendship, along with many others, so had had no cause to attach particular importance to the relationship, that is until that meeting took place. We took to Else Marie immediately; her friendliness and easy going charm, her dark good looks and the warmth of her welcome captivated and made a lasting impression. However it was to be some time before she became one of the family, this friendship we were told was purely platonic and we, as English guests were welcomed and given a view of Norwegian family life free from ulterior motive.

Gunnar Lervik was approaching 70, a retired tailor who now devoted his energies to fishing and gardening, Inger, younger by several years, still worked as an assistant in an old people's home, and had also brought up a family of five, four brothers to Else Marie, all but one of whom were now away from home. The house had the true hallmark of a much-loved family home. Abundant is a word that best describes the style of furnishing, not in an ostentatious way, in fact the furniture, though comfortable is fairly plain but there's a lot of it. But the lace curtains potted plants, framed needlework pictures, bunches of garden flowers, and many family photographs are what give the singular national characteristic.

Gunnar's garden was that of a true countryman, an impeccably kept, well-stocked kitchen garden. He took great pleasure in giving us a guided tour of the serried rows of potatoes, onions, beet and green stuff of all kinds, but the pleasure was ours when we sat down to lunch at the table crammed with the fruits of his labour. This was something like the Good Life, not only home produced vegetables and fruit but fish too caught from Gunnar's own small boat. The dish was a very tasty fish pie baked with a mixture of herbs and small pasta and lots of butter that went by the name of fiskegrateng. Fish for the islanders is the staple diet but according to Robert the excellent basic material can be ruined by thrifty housewives who insist on messing it about, never serving it as fried steaks or fillets as in the preferred manner back home. I personally approve the novel differences and sympathise with the need to make a little go a long way when there are many mouths to feed.

The afternoon was spent swimming and sunbathing at a lovely quiet sandy beach. This was Breivika, a silver crescent edging a crystal clear lagoon formed by rocky islets and a sheltering headland. We learned later that a NATO communications mast was sighted in the vicinity and the locals believed that Russian trawlers used to sit out in the fjord, eavesdropping for state secrets, whenever the wind blew in their direction. The place was also used as the setting for an espionage novel that became a best seller locally, 'Origo' by Kim Småge. Espionage and Russian spies and state secrets could not have been further from our minds on that beautiful, remote, island beach.

Retrospection is an indulgence that frequently gives rise to delusive memories. The tendency is for the good to be very good and the bad to be denied altogether. Who has never been guilty of professing that the sun always shone in the good old days when summers really were summers? With this in mind I am prompted to set down that for me beautiful Breivika had its darker side, a painful consequence brought about by vanity of the competitive kind. The sea may have been crystal clear but it was cold and to warm up after swimming, a race along the sands was proposed and this was my downfall. I forgot to be my age, tore along as though a national gold medal was as stake and bang, back came the sciatica. Pride certainly brought about that particular fall.

The Lervik family refused to consider the possibility that we should take the early ferry back to Molde, there was still the ceremony of tea, without which no Norwegian social visit can be deemed to be a success. Again the table groaned with a surfeit of eye-catching and mouth-watering goodies, smørbrød with all kinds of meat, cheese, fish and salad, followed by bowls of soft fruits and a selection of richly luscious cream cakes. Admonished to eat our fill, we learnt a Norwegian expression that was to be reiterated countless times at many such offerings in the years ahead: Det er mer på kjøkkenet. There's more in the kitchen.

Although language was a barrier to a close relationship or understanding, this was overcome to a great extent by mutual goodwill and the warm hospitality both given and received. Robert and Else Marie worked sympathetically as interpreters, creating the foundations on which a lasting rapport came to be established. Inger and her munificent table often returned to us in vivid recall, particularly when lean times pinched somewhat, as they undoubtedly did at times. This beginning was something of a fool's paradise, but it served well as a buffer from which to rebound along an entirely unknown track: the Zen track that has no goal, a travelling without point with nowhere to go.

The time had come when we could test the old cliché, 'To travel well is better than to arrive', for we had only the vaguest notions of route let alone destination. However, preparations must be made. The Lancia underwent drastic

21

reorganisation and was made ready for whatever lay ahead and then came the painful business of goodbyes. It was the usual confusion of emotional part sentences, irrelevant questions, exhortations to write, a nervous void with everything and yet nothing to say.

And then it was over with Vestnes behind us, a half-remembered dream, the only reality the road ahead and the next place name on the map. To reach Oslo in time for the morning ferry to Denmark meant driving through the night, a journey of about ten hours. Although it was over a month since the summer solstice, nights were still quite short with few dark hours separating a lingering twilight from a pearly dawn. Because of night's brevity, activity amongst nocturnal animals was highly concentrated. The road seemed to attract all kinds of creatures who scurried across the twin beams from the headlights intent on their own individual needs and destinations, extra vigilance was necessary to avoid cutting them down. Unwittingly they were of service to us by helping to keep us alert during the dangerous small hours when sleep threatened, for these creatures of the night were our only diversion on the otherwise deserted road for the greater part of the journey.

Not surprisingly, we were tired out by the time we reached Oslo's sea terminal. We were in good time with a couple of hours to spare before the departure, scheduled for nine o'clock, and the prospect of a seven-hour crossing in which to recuperate sustained us. Then the blow fell. Sailing cancelled, stated a stark notice, not this time on account of industrial action as had so nearly happened in the Isle of Man, this was engine failure. The single vessel that served this route was suffering from overwork, and we were well and truly snookered.

At a loss, we faced each other on the deserted quay, trying ineffectually to come up with a positive solution to the predicament. If only there was someone to share the problem, someone of whom we might ask advice. There was nothing to be gleaned from the cryptic notice of cancellation. Then as if in answer to our supplication a man approached. A coloured man, exceedingly dark skinned and of stocky figure, intensely bright intelligent eyes and an encouraging smile, but best of all was his response to our overtures – in English. He was a stevedore in the port of Oslo and when we explained the situation he suggested that we should make enquiries as to the possible alternatives at the office of the Danish ferry company, when it opened at 8 o'clock, and told us how to find it. The business out of the way and relieved to have a course to follow we chatted amiably with our benefactor for a few minutes. He came from Goa, the tiny colony belonging to Portugal on the West Coast of India and to add further to his quality of cosmopolitanism, he was married to a Danish woman. Our Sir Galahad was quite an enigma, one lone dark Asiatic amongst a race of tall fair Vikings.

Following our Goan friend's advice we found the requisite office where we learned of an alternative route to Frederikshavn from the port of Fredrikstad, sixty miles south-east of Oslo. A boat was due to leave at five o'clock in the afternoon, an interminable interval, or so it seemed after the all night drive. We found a café open where coffee and toast went some way to fortifying us, at least it was enough to spark off a modicum of initiative to explore the adjacent area of Oslo, given this unlooked for opportunity. My impressions are far from clear, fogged no doubt by a web of fatigue. That it was unaccountably hot I remember well. If this was Norway what would it be like in Italy we wondered, but this was one of those meteorological flukes, we learned later that on that 5th day of August 1982 Oslo was the hottest city in Europe.

So, what with the heat and fatigue we did not get very far. A walk along the grand boulevard Karl Johan Gate with its many open-air restaurants, deserted at this early hour, led us to a pleasant open space, a kind of unfenced park where we collapsed onto an inviting tree-shaded seat. There, within a stone's throw of our haven, on a slight rise to our left we saw a classic ochre-yellow building familiar from guidebooks, the royal palace. King Olave was well known for his refusal to distance himself and his family from his people and this use of the palace grounds as a public park gave credence to the stories told about him.

It was useless to press on any further so sightseeing curtailed, we drifted back to the car and slowly made our way to the alternative port of embarkation. It was impossible to make sixty miles last all day however delicate the foot on the accelerator and this meant more time to kill at the other end. We found a place to eat and afterwards forced our weary reluctant bodies to drag around the old quarter of the port, one of Norway's famous living museums. We saw much that was of interest in the quaint old timbered buildings and had we been more compos mentis our appreciation would have been greater. As it was we would never see it again for the following year fire destroyed the greater part of old Fredrikstad with its beautiful timber houses.

After an uncomfortable wait in the broiling unshaded embarkation queue, we eventually found ourselves aboard and for some reason having to wrangle over cabin reservations. By this time our tempers were badly frayed and in no state for any further procrastination. Tickets were in order clearly stating cabin reservations but apparently, the change of route and vessel was the cause of the trouble, which, with some determined perseverance on our part was solved satisfactorily. We had a place to lie down and forget the frustrations of the day. But first it was necessary to eat and this meant queuing again although the end product was hardly worth the trouble, the standards of food and service fell far short of those we had enjoyed on the M.V.ENGLAND. We really believed that our day of adversity was over but there was more to come, the sequel happened as we approached Denmark, with yet an hour to disembarkation.

We were asleep, both of us dead to the world when a loud and persistent knocking dragged us from the depths of unconsciousness, and this was accompanied by an equally loud and unintelligible voice outside the door. What could be wrong? was the ship sinking? was this a nightmare? Along such lines ran my sleep-fogged thoughts, until the door burst open and the light went on. For an infinitesimal moment silence reigned followed by the sudden departure of the inter-loper who then continued shouting from beyond the door. By this time, we were fully awake, and one look at Eric still pros-trate on the upper bunk explained the strange behaviour of the uninvited visitor. He was naked, having dispensed with any covering in the humid heat of the confined cabin, hence the rapid exit. We gradually got the gist of the continued harassment. It was an hour yet before midnight, arrival time, and we were being ejected, thrown out of our hard won cabin with sleep still making its persistent demands. As we left, the stewardess, looking to our eyes more like a wardress, glow-ered as though we were guilty of some heinous crime when all we wanted in the world was sleep.

The remainder of the night is a confusion of disem-barkation and driving away, only vaguely aware that the road led out of town. It was not long before a generous lay-by tempted us off the road and without even bothering to climb into sleeping bags we reclined the seats and were immediate-ly out for the count.

That was the end of the holiday. Henceforth each day was an unknown quantity the only common factor being the inexorable movement towards the south. This was the thresh-old to our New World, the culmination of a year of vague dreams and now at last the realisation was within reach.

Chapter Three

Southbound

'I travelled among unknown men in lands beyond the sea'
                                                    Wordsworth.

There is no luxurious lazy awakening from car-sleep. No turning over and going off again. You wake from fitful sleep at the first glimmer of daylight and the only relief from cramped and aching muscles is to extricate yourself, stagger outside and limber up gradually into some semblance of mobility. Incredibly, the lay-by stumbled upon in the dead of night, turned out to be a well equipped picnic area including landscaped arbours, rustic furniture, a fresh water supply, and best of all, a tolerably clean lavatory. It was all very civilised and together with the finest of summer mornings it proved the perfect antidote for the tribulations of the previous twenty-four hours. Fortified by a hearty breakfast of Norwegian bread and gudbrandsdal cheese followed by English marmalade and tea we were ready to face whatever challenge the new day in 'terra incognita' might bring.

From Denmark to Italy by way of Germany and Austria was to take us five days, by no means a record break-ing achievement but that was not the object of the exercise. Had our main concern been to get from A to B in half that time it could easily have been done but without half the actu-al interest. To fly across Europe using autobahns and autoroutes is all very well if one is content with nothing other that speeding traffic. On such roads it is usually my fate to be sandwiched between monstrous juggernauts with nothing but high grassed banks on either hand, not in my view the most inspiring mode of movement. It can be argued that minor roads are not so well surfaced and also that cross country routes may lead to navigational difficulties but there is no disputing that they invariably give a closer view of the foreign scene, and that was our 'raison d'être'.

This new country that unfolded around us was not so very different from a southern English landscape: rolling fertile fields, extensive woods, river valleys, skyline windmills, and red brick villages. There was none of the spectacular drama of Norway's scenery but the calm simplicity and easier roads suited our mood after the telling extremes of the previous day.

We drove into Hadeslev, in the heart of the lovely East Jutland countryside just as we were beginning to feel the need of a square meal. It was a good place to pause awhile. Criss-crossed by a network of canals and with a fine legacy of well preserved ancient houses it looked well worth investigating, but first we must eat. It was market day in Hadeslev with all the hurly-burly that is synonymous with market days the world over: the crush of traffic, bustling crowds and a general buzz of sound that was not unpleasant after the silence of the early morning drive. We found a cafe overlooking the centre of action, the Market Square, where we lunched well on roast chicken and salad and a delectable sweet pastry desert. First-aid food supply was next on the agenda, a precaution we made a point of taking as we could not be sure of what might lie ahead, and the only other purchase we made was a replacement for sunglasses left behind on a cross-fjord ferry somewhere in Norway. The chores out of the way it was time to turn tourist.

The highlight of a pleasant hour wandering round that most attractive town was coming across the impressive Gothic cathedral. The name Hadeslev had a vaguely familiar ring but it was not until we entered the Domkirch that we realised why. A notice giving details of a series of organ recitals gave the answer. It so happened that several of these recitals had been broadcast on BBC radio 3 and we had listened to these, innocent of the fact that by sheer coincidence Hadeslev would be our first port of call on this haphazard journey. We were not to have the pleasure of hearing the renowned organ on this visit but it was well worth viewing, a magnificent example of the architectural skill of the organ builder that is a part of yet separate from the musical technicalities. The towering gilded pipes and ornate scrolls led the eye upwards to the great vaulting, 72 feet over the floor of the nave, the tallest church in Scandinavia.

Refreshed by this pleasant interlude we resumed the journey. The thirty miles to the frontier were quickly covered and we crossed into Germany to readjust to yet another language and another currency. As the afternoon wore on there was a subtle change in the atmosphere, light cloud hid the sun that had been our constant companion since sailing into Oslo, and gradually as the sky darkened it became obvious that we were in for a storm. It broke with ear-shattering violence. Incessant thunder and lightning accompanied by torrential rain made driving conditions intolerable but there was nowhere to stop. With extreme caution, we kept going hoping for a village or a wayside inn to emerge from the aqueous world. We sailed into Tarp, a village roughly mid-way between Flensburg and Schleswig, and squelched our way to beg shelter at the only inn. To our relief, they had a room, our first 'zimmer und fruhstuck' and at fifty marks (the current rate of exchange was about 4.5 to the £), we felt we had struck beginners luck. Subsequently we were to find this to be the going rate along the entire German and Austrian route, excellent standard and value throughout.

It was now Saturday August 7th, just twelve days from leaving Manx shores but it might have been twelve months or even years, it seemed so remote. The new routine of perpetual movement, while still novel, did not in any way appear to be irregular. To have the Fulvia's wheels spinning along another new road on another day was the very essence of living. The storm clouds had passed over leaving a newly washed, scintillating world under a faultless blue sky. Fields of ochre-coloured grain ripe for harvesting rolled away on either hand, giving way at intervals to tracts of deep shaded woodland or exceedingly neat villages and towns. Progress was smooth and uneventful during the morning with moderate traffic and no navigational hitches, but early in the afternoon we joined an interminable tailback of crawling vehicles. To begin with, it was impossible to discover the cause of the hold-up. The road was narrow, level and straight at this point but when a bend in the road gave a longer view the sight was not reassuring. We were following in the wake of an army on the move, a slow moving military convoy that stretched away into infinity, or so it seemed, with all the time in the world to get where they were going. By degrees the group of khaki-coloured lorries were overhauled by intervening traffic, we crept closer and at last our turn came. This was the difficult bit. It was tedious hopping our way to the head of the convoy with hardly a break in the oncoming stream of vehicles but what a wonderful feeling of release when we finally made it. There ahead was the longed for open road and like a greyhound freed from the slips, the Fulvia seemed to surge ahead almost of her own volition.

Shortly afterwards in Saltzgitter-Bad, concentration must have lapsed at a crucial moment, at a vital intersection, and we were thrown off course. This minor mistake actually turned to our advantage. It led to the beautiful region of the Hartz mountains and the village of Leibenburg where we chose to stop for the night. The only inn turned out to be full much to our disappointment; it might be miles to another suitable stopping place. But we had reckoned without this country landlord's ingenuity. He waved us back, made a brief telephone call and contrived through sign language and a great deal of gesticulation to make us understand that he had arranged for us to stay privately in the village. He then took the trouble to show us the way and even offered, or rather insisted on ferrying us to and from the inn for 'abendessen'. We needed little persuasion. We were hungry and our appetites were stimulated further by tantalising cooking smells wafting from the kitchen.

The house in which we found ourselves was a neat modern villa with a small but equally precise garden ablaze with flowers of high summer. Our room was a delight and made us feel like honoured guests. It had a most comfortable feather mattress, lavender scented duvet and pillows and a luxurious en suite bathroom. So much for my boast of lean times ahead and shoestring travel!

Back at the picturesque 17th century inn, we dined 'al fresco' in an old walled garden scented with lavender and stocks and full-blown roses. The meal of tender veal steaks and fresh vegetables followed by apfel strudel quite lived up to its promise. The innkeeper's wife who served our meal spoke a little English, acquired during a spell working in London and the Shropshire town of Whitchurch. It had been a very happy period of her life she told us and now she was glad to welcome English visitors to her home whenever the chance arose. This explained our reception, the lengths to which her husband had gone to accommodate and welcome us.

The next morning, Leibenburg's friendly hospitality continued. The table at breakfast groaned beneath a veritable banquet of wursts, cheeses, eggs, preserves of every conceivable kind, a choice of home baked breads and huge pots of coffee and tea. There was enough to feed a large family and when we capitulated with a great deal left untouched, our indefatigable Frau packed all that remained in case we should feel hungry on our journey. The bill was again only 50mks. Yet, the entire episode merited at least five stars in our book.

Before leaving the village, we took a walk to have a closer look at an example of a working Domaine noticed as we entered Leibenburg on the previous day. It was a complete unit of manor house, labourer's cottages, cattle sheds stables, and the whole dominated by an immense granary. It was grouped with the customary German sense of order and cleanliness around an open square, part grass and part cobblestone paving. We saw many of these quaint and antique domaines but none to match the splendour of this one.

We left for Gottingen soon after nine and set about locating the elusive route 27 but again something went wrong and again we found ourselves touring the Hartz mountains.

Yes this was route 27, it was plainly indicated on the kilometre posts but we could not pinpoint the position on the map. Now, even though the surroundings are beautiful the attraction palls when you are lost and seem condemned to drive forever just off the map. The light dawned when we found ourselves alongside the East German border somewhere in Thuringia, miles from where we ought to have been. It was such a simple mistake, obvious once it is exposed. We were travelling on the correct road in the wrong direction.

By the time we found ourselves the road was running alongside a high barbed-wire fence watched over by armed guards in observation posts placed at regular intervals. This was the great east/west divide that at that time appeared insurmountable for who could envisage the cataclysmic way in which the situation was resolved. The hostile spectacle quite overshadowed the bright summer morning.

One and a half-hours or sixty miles was the cost of the morning's extra tour, an insignificant miscalculation that was forgotten as soon as Gottingen was behind us and we were southbound once again. However, two false moves on consecutive days made us rather more careful and considerably more map conscious. Without further incident, stopping only to eat a picnic lunch courtesy of our Liebenburg hostess, we pressed on for a little over 200 miles of fairly unremarkable country before calling a halt at a wayside hotel between Fulda and Hammelburg. Once more, it seemed as though we had only to voice the idea that we'd had enough driving and were in need of respite for a likely source to present itself. I liked to think that old Hermes, the ancient God of travellers was keeping a kindly eye on our progress. As with the previous ports of call, every aspect was faultless and again the day ended idyllically with supper out of doors, this time on a terrace looking over a green landscape steeped in the rays of a low, full-blown westering sun.

Monday August 9th. According to the map, we were now following the 'Romantic Route', a misnomer to my jaundiced eye as the scenery of the early miles was nothing but bland acres and acres of dust-green maize. I was feeling low this morning. Three and a half days of restricted movement was beginning to take its toll, the old sciatic hip was playing up and consequently I was hardly in an appreciative frame of mind. I dosed myself with aspirin and then we tried a little mental therapy imagining the pleasures of walking in Tuscany, of bathing at some sunny lakeside resort in Austria or Italy. We talked about the difficult experiences endured by travellers of the past; writers and artists, poets and scholars, all drawn inexorably to Italy and the Mediterranean, the cradle of civilisation in the west. Some made their way on foot, others on horseback or by diligence, perhaps along this very road. It was an idea that appealed and one that might explain the charismatic name the 'Romantic Route'.

At what juncture, the maize gave way to a more varied landscape I am unable to state categorically but we were suddenly aware that the aspect had altered. With a thrill of excitement it was noted that the road had started to undulate with the emphasis on the upward trend, we were approaching the alpine crossing. With the ascent there came a wonderful series of scene changes that followed each other with amazing variety; Arcadian landscapes of smooth emerald-velvet meadows, dark coniferous forests rising to rocky heights and pinnacles, clear mountain torrents racing through confined gorges or meandering through lush water meadows. We passed painted farms almost glossy with perfection, hamlets so spick and span they looked absurdly unreal and even the cows grazing in the florescent fields were almost too good to be true, they shone like porcelain in the brilliant mountain air.

As we climbed, the road grew more and more congested and the reason for this became obvious when the map revealed that Oberammergau of Passion Play fame lay directly ahead. Being as inquisitive as the next man we speculated as to our chances of overnighting in this world renowned Alpine village, but finding ourselves flung headlong into the confusion of full-scale tourism we promptly changed our minds. It was hard to believe that this was not the year of the plays such were the traffic snarl-ups, choked car parks, and teeming cosmopolitan crowds thronging in and out of endless gift shops. It was all very bewildering. Above the razzle-dazzle on the streets, the local architecture played its part in the scheme of things with an indulgence of theatrical-like wall frescos on pastoral and religious themes. It was all just too much and passing yet another queue of hapless motorists waiting for a suitable slot we willingly journeyed on.

In less than a dozen miles lady luck turned up trumps again as we drew up at the gate of a small guest house on a peaceful street in Oberau. It was the perfect antithesis of Oberammagau from the human angle even though its situation and physical aspects were comparable. There was no problem in securing a room or finding space for the car and that done we went in search of somewhere to eat. An inn soon presented itself and we went inside. It was busy, but a cheerful looking waitress carrying a large fully loaded tray was not too busy to take the trouble to find seats for us at a communal table. It really was quite miraculous the way in which that one waitress kept a large roomful of hungry patrons supplied with food and drink. They were a mixed bunch, of all ages and from various levels of society, all shoulder to shoulder round large tables with one common intent, to enjoy themselves. At the adjacent table to ours sat a party of leather breeched, tyrolean hatted men who by the sound of things had already imbibed a fair quantity of the ale that came to the tables foaming in great tankards, litres I suppose. They kept up a constant repartee with the waitress and with each other which might have been rowdy if it hadn't been so apparently good-natured. Anyway, we had no way of knowing what the jokes were about nevertheless found ourselves caught up by the convivial atmosphere. The jollity was infectious and we soon shrugged off all traces of travel fatigue, aided no doubt by a good meal of country stew and a robust local wine. A keen appetite and novel surroundings made high spots of those evening meals whether alone in a garden or in such a situation as this.

The departure next morning from Oberau was delayed. Immediate family had extracted promises for periodic information as to our whereabouts and the time had come for the first dispatch. Six communications dutifully written we had to locate a post office and this presented difficulties, not insuperable but quite time consuming and frustrating trying to follow directions in an unfamiliar language. It is at times like this that you realise how transitory is the quest for freedom, absolute freedom which in reality is a sensuous myth that we delude ourselves into believing possible. In the end, as with most things in life, it all boils down to compromise and one must make the most of the graspable parts.

When we did eventually get away we ran almost immediately into heavy traffic, the worst so far and to cap it all it came on to rain. Driving in convoy on torturous mountain roads is never easy but with wet roads and streaming windscreen, it is even more onerous. And at this critical moment, the windscreen wipers chose to malfunction. A sporadic judder and swish was the best they could manage and it was simply not good enough to cope with the conditions. It was grim but there was nothing we could do about it but try to cling on to the rear lights of the car ahead and will the foul weather to cease. We came through it at last and the release of our joint tension was audible, like escaping gas from a deflating balloon. We made a mental note to attend to the fault at the earliest opportunity. All being well we should be in Italy tonight, or tomorrow at the latest and there should be no obstacle to obtaining first aid for our trusty steed in the land of her origin.

During the climb up from Oberau, the road had divided giving a choice of two routes, the Brenner Pass which seemed the more popular taking the bulk of traffic, or the lesser but more circuitous Fern Pass which was the one for which we opted. There was no let up from dealing with hairpin bends but at least the flow of traffic was a great deal less that the earlier climb, so giving one the option to choose ones own pace. The valiant Fulvia tacked and veered her way up and round each successive bend, up the steep gradient almost as though she could 'smell the stables', and like her drivers would not be opposed to a few days respite on the shores of Lake Garda.

Along the way the frontier of Austria was unobtrusively crossed, a bored looking official waving us on with scarcely so much as a glance. I suppose we must have anticipated a more rigorous checking of luggage and passport with an official rubber stamp of authorisation before being allowed through. One almost regretted the trouble free crossing that seemed in a way to detract from the great adventure of travel.

Fern Pass safely negotiated, we passed through Landeck and over a second, though considerably less severe Resia Pass and down at last into Italy. At this point, we were almost too tired to appreciate this significant arrival but we looked forward to tomorrow and were quietly happy. The disillusion was yet to come. It was early evening of what had turned into a brilliant day that we entered Riva and could scarcely believe what we found. The pretty lakeside resort was bursting at the seams, seething masses of humanity making the memory of Oberammergau a haven of tranquillity by comparison, for it had apparently been invaded by youthful German wind-surfers here in their thousands in the hope of conquering world sailing titles. This week turned out to be the peak of both the German and Italian holiday seasons and to find a room, or even a place to stop the car was a physical impossibility. Every street was choked, every window sported a 'completo' sign, and with spirits at a very low ebb we inched a tortuous way out of the maelstrom and made for Torbole. Here we met exactly the same situation, and at Malcesine too, it was hopeless. Back we trailed to the head of the lake and in desperation took a higher road that lead into the hills. At least there would be no windsurfers up there and we might find a suitable spot to stop and eat our dry bread and cheese, and as a last resort sleep in the car.

In the event, we avoided such extremities. Albergo Rosa Alpina at Stumiago hidden away in the forested hills above Lake Garda had a vacancy. At least a decent night's sleep was assured but being early closing day, the restaurant was not functioning which left the question of how to keep the wolf from the door. We were desperately hungry. Supper eventually turned out to be coffee and sandwiches, or rather 'cappuccino and prosciuttoo panini' at a bar in a campsite a short distance along the road. Not the greatest introduction to our chosen Promised Land but it sufficed and could have been considerably worse. When you are as tired as we were that night anticlimax is inevitable even given reasonable circumstances and that arrival could hardly be described as reasonable. The dawn of a new day restored good humour and renewed enthusiasm for the expedition and as we hit the road that was fragrant with thyme and warm earth and foliage, the smell of Italy, we felt optimistic, convinced that today would be a good day.

It was decided that we abandon Garda altogether and try our luck at the smaller less well known Lake Iseo to the west. It was pleasant driving along the hill road so cool and green, shaded by chestnut and pine with occasional glimpses of the shimmering lake below and then we plunged back into the mainstream traffic on the approach to Brescia. It was not too bad though as we were soon to break away again for Iseo town and the eastern shore of the delightful gem of a lake. The gamble had paid off for here the traffic was lighter, towns far less frenetic and although the scenery was not quite so spectacular as the Great Lakes it was still very beautiful.

A small spit of land jutting into the lake offered itself as an ideal place to take stock while the kettle boiled for coffee. This would definitely 'do' we decided, it was the most perfect spot for a short recuperation period if only we might find a place to stay.

And that was when Sergio appeared. He strolled over towards, what to him would be a perfectly familiar Italian car, and stopped at sight of the GBM nationality identification letters, the Manx version of the customary GB sticker. This had already attracted a few curious glances and was now an opening gambit that turned greatly to our advantage. We endeavoured to explain the origin of the mysterious GBM - although shaky, our attempts at communicating in Italian were rather better than any of the Teutonic languages and a delighted Sergio responded in equally shaky English telling us that he once met a girl from 'Isola di Man' when working in Kenya. He was also quite 'au fait' with the Manx Tourist Trophy motor-bike races - the famous T.T.- which had been won on many occasions in the '60s' by the glamorous and fearless hero of every Italian enthusiast, Giacomo Agostini.

We told him about our wish to stay a while in the vicinity and asked his advice and his response was immediate. We were invited over the road to his business premises, a small leather works, where one of his employees was delegated to act as a guide to a very good cheap hotel that he could recommend with all his heart. It probably belonged to a cousin or brother-in-law or some other relative but be that as it may, we could not have improved upon it by chance. Before leaving to follow our Vespa-mounted guide, we were given a guided tour around the factory and received a parting gift of a pocket note-case each. Sergio should have been an ambassador or diplomat for I felt sure he could have cemented the flimsiest of international relations. We never saw him again but his welcome and practical help on this our first day in Italy was a reassuring human gesture that is not easily forgotten.

Hotel Master at Sulzano was small and friendly and situated right at the edge of the lake, perfect for our needs, the long anticipated opening chapter of the Italian experience. The lake itself although one of the smallest in the northern lakeland group, at fifteen and a half miles long is hardly insignificant. It contains the largest lake island in Italy, Monte Isola which rises to an impressive 1,965 feet and is six miles in circumference, and it so happened that the only ferry giving access to this intriguing island was only a few minutes away from Hotel Master.

In retrospect, it seems perverse that despite all these advantages we actually found it hard at first to relax and simply enjoy doing nothing. It must have been a case of traveller's sickness when the patient cannot shrug off the need for perpetual motion, the subconscious has grown accustomed to movement and is irritated by the lack of it, so relaxation is inhibited. There was also the growing awareness of our homeless condition, self imposed though it was, apprehension rose to the surface periodically during the probationary period.

However, the Italian sun soon worked its magic together with the tranquil surroundings and a less impetuous mood prevailed accepting what the moment had to offer. We walked and bathed, read and wrote letters dividing the time between the lakeside hotel garden and the other world across the water, the charming and quite irresistible island. It was virtually traffic free making it ideal for walking and picnics, whether the mood demanded an energetic circumambulation or a gentle stroll through shady olive groves. The fish restaurants in the diminutive harbour tempted us back several times to indulge in the local speciality, the delicate flavoured lake fish of amazing variety, of all shapes sizes and colours. Cooked to perfection, it was a dish worthy of the highest accolade.

On the fourth morning at Sulzano we decided to investigate the entire circumference of the lake and take a closer look at the clustering red-roofed towns at the foot of the mountains on the opposite shore. It was time to rouse the Lancia from her fully deserved rest but before setting out Eric made a few routine checks in the usual way: oil and water levels, wash windscreen, lights etc. And all seemed to be in order until we came to start the engine. All was silence, no response; it absolutely refused to fire. Then it was that the memory of the faltering windscreen wipers on the alpine crossing returned giving the clue to the problem. The battery was flat and beyond redemption, drained by a metal clip of a strap that Eric had used to secure tools under the bonnet. Being a small car, stowing space was valuable and it had seemed a pity to waste so much spare area under the bonnet, but this ad-hoc system proved rather costly. Apparently, the offending clip had come into contact with the circuit controlling the windscreen wipers, slowing it down and consequently draining the battery. The hotel padrone came to our rescue with a telephone call to the local service station. Within an hour a mechanic arrived with a new battery, the car found her voice again and was pronounced fit and well and we ruefully paid the fifty-pound bill.

Enthusiasm for the excursion had waned a little during Fulvia's crisis but we finally got under way. And then we met such perilous driving conditions, we had grave doubts about the sanity of the enterprise and I secretly wished myself back in Hotel Master's delightful garden. The road, a corniche hugging the lakeshore at the foot of precipitous cliffs could be compared to a grand-prix circuit. A constant stream of hair raisingly fast cars hurtled by, which would have been fine had the road been a fraction wider and had there not been another such race being run in the opposite direction. These must surely be the sons of the historic Mille Miglia, the celebrated road race that ended in disaster and was subsequently banned being declared too dangerous even for this nation of volatile drivers.

A period of calm descended during siesta and we passed through the two industrial towns of Pisogne and Lovere at the northern tip of the lake. From here conditions improved, the traffic almost disappeared and we were able to appreciate the new vistas offered by the western shore, high mountains reflected in still waters, luxuriant vegetation and all bathed in the ambience of clear and brilliant light. We revelled in the heat. The close proximity of water and the soft air from the mountains mitigated its fiercer effects and gradually, pale northern complexions had turned to warm brown. It was fun to look upon 'our' island from a different angle and to prolong the experience we ordered ice cream at a pavement cafe directly opposite to Sulzano. Unfortunately we forgot to specify 'small' and were almost overwhelmed by the huge concoctions that were ceremoniously placed before us. But they were delicious and easily dealt with.

There were no other English tourists at our hotel so social exchange was fairly limited until that is the penultimate evening. At the adjacent table to ours in the dining room, we had exchanged greetings several times with a German couple, and on this particular night, it happened that we left the room at the same time. Pleasantries ensued and we joined forces for coffee where identities were established. They introduced themselves as Heinz and Heide, from Ulm in West Germany and told us that they were regulars at Hotel Master, which suited their needs ideally. They approved of the quiet comfort, the scenery, the weather, but above all, they came for the water sport, or at least Heinz did. He was a fit athletic looking 50 year old of the gregarious type who had a definite penchant for water, he was either swimming in it or windsurfing on it for the greater part of each day. Heide on the other hand appeared to be rather introspective, the exact opposite of her husband, preferring to sit alone with a book during Heinz' energetic waterborne hours. Following a shared stroll on the waterfront, our new friends introduced us to Captain's Bar, a scruffy little place hidden away in a dark corner by the ferry that oozed character. One often reads of such establishments but rarely comes across by chance, and but for this encounter it would have gone by unnoticed.

Life stories were soon being related over a mellow wine called Tokia. A wine the colour of liquid sunlight and an unimpeachable flavour that called forth animation and good cheer. Heinz grew quite loquacious, he was a natural raconteur and enjoyed airing his fluent, but sometimes inaccurate English, while Heide, though reticent was able to correct his grammatical 'faux pas'. For instance, when talking of their early history he used the expression 'If we were married' and was blushingly corrected with a low, 'you should say when we were married. It was a delightful evening, one of those rare moments of pure happiness, enfolded in the warm velvet night, the darkness throbbing with the hypnotic stridulations of cicadas, while from over the water another kind of music from some village festa drifted on the still air to harmonise with the rhythmic slap of waves against the jetty.

It was a brief idyll. The German pair were due to leave for home the very next day, and our own rest period was almost at an end, we planned to proceed with the Italian journey on the day following. So the usual hopes that we would meet again were exchanged and we said goodbye.

The preparations for departure were accompanied by the threat of storm. All day the air was heavy and stiflingly close, an enervating day that only came alive when the storm finally broke later in the afternoon. It was a dramatic setting for such an elemental tumult with almost continuous flashes of lightning reflected in the glass-like surface of the lake and reverberating thunder claps bouncing between the encircling mountains. Then came the squall wind to shatter the mirror smooth waters and transform them into a sea of furious waves. It was difficult to concentrate on packing with so much energy and violence going on without pause. In the morning a broken masted yacht drifted slowly by, a sobering reminder of the destructive power of these mountain storms.

It was good to be on the road again, the Fulvia once more our home, the hub of our daily life. The sky was still overcast, the road steely grey and wet from the nights rain, but by mid-day as we crossed the flat plain of the river Po, we left the cloud behind hanging shroud-like between us and the Alps, the barrier that separates north from south. It was almost symbolic, like a door closing on a previous existence. No looking back now, only ahead to face whatever pitfalls and frustrations there might be intermingled with the undoubted pleasures of such a journey.

During the preceding days we had spent some time studying the map to give some shape and purpose to the next stage, nothing too rigid of course, freedom and flexibility were talismanic guides on which we set great store. And now the whole of Italy lay before us, a tempting casket of treasures to be selected as and when we fancied. The great problem was choosing, where should we begin?

Chapter Four

Adrift: The Euphoria and Misgivings

What master of the pencil or the style had traced the shades and lines?

(Divine Comedy - Dante)

'Ravenna, former imperial city, Byzantium of the west, wrapped in nostalgic charm and containing the finest and richest evidences of early Christian art; its mosaics alone are worth a journey.' Such is the Green Guide's laudatory tribute that was principally responsible for determining our initial direction. It was not out of our way to take in the celebrated mosaics as there was no pre-planned way to be taken out of and as things turned out it was a valuable decision.

It was during siesta time that we drove into an uncannily silent city, sweltering in the throes of a high summer heat wave. Searing light alternated with deep shadow steeped in somnolence, not even a town pigeon disturbed the inert air. It was not the ideal time for sightseeing but with a reserve of energy resulting from the lakeland sojourn and a certain naive rashness, we refused to be put off. There was the inevitable question of where to park, every street being lined already with dusty vehicles that looked as though they had been there since the beginning of time, Then, with a tremendous stroke of luck we came upon, not only a vacant slot but a tree-shaded one, a rare and greatly prized amenity in the fierce light of the August sun. Because of the advanced hour the initial itinerary would have to be restricted to only two, or possibly three of the principal mosaics and on checking our bearings we plumped for the Aryan Baptistry followed by the church of San Vitale with the Mausoleum of Galla Placidia if time and energy permitted.

Following the Green guide's street map we soon found the Baptistry, hidden away in a small cobbled piazza, but to our acute disappointment, it was locked. One of a small group of workmen squatting in the shadow of the old walls, indicated his wristwatch and muttered the word 'chiuso' reminding us that we were too early. Of course we had clean forgotten that everything stops during siesta, and we silently cursed the loss of an afternoon of the 'finest and richest evidences of early Christian art'. Drinks at a piazza bar (presuming we could find one) seemed a poor substitute for our high intentions. As we hesitated uncertain what to do next an elderly rugged looking man hurried across the piazza towards us brandishing a huge key. It was the custodian himself and ignoring the regulation opening time he happily ushered us forward, turned the key in the massive old lock, pushed open the great door and we were inside.

It was a few minutes before sun-dazzled eyes adjusted to the subdued light of the cool dim interior and our accommodating mentor drew attention upwards to the cupola. There was the object of renown that brought so many devotees to this spot to contemplate and admire. The cupola is lined with a shimmering depiction of the Baptism of Christ, the central design made up of three figures John the Baptist on the right, Christ immersed in the waters of the river Jordan in the centre with the allegorical divinity of water on the left. The blue, green and skin tones of the small irregular blocks (tesserae) that compose the mosaic are incredibly pure and clearly defined against a glittering background of gold, all as fresh as new paint. To complete the domed design a circle of processing white-robed apostles frames the three central figures serving to emphasise their consequence. Despite the subdued light filtering into the old building, the entire cupola seemed aglow with an internal illumination, a hidden source of power.

It was a rewarding curtain raiser, a memorable private viewing with which we were well satisfied and for which we were anxious to give tangible appreciation to our guide. It wasn't easy. The old man showed great reluctance to accept a small gratuity, a thousand lire I think it was, but finally took the note with profuse thanks and we parted company.

Back in the blazing heat of the street we felt like Noel Coward's mad Englishmen, the Italians apparently not caring to, and no one else daring to venture out in the mid-day sun even for such rewards as these. On the way to the second site, the Galla Placidia, we first came to the tomb of Dante, Italy's greatest poet. It is said that in 1321, because of his enforced exile from his beloved Florence, city of his birth, he died here in Ravenna of a broken heart. Sometime during his life, perhaps when there was still hope of reprieve, he apparently found some consolation in the mosaics in the city of his detention for he includes a reference to them in his Divine Comedy calling them 'symphonies of colour'.

The Mausoleum of Galla Placidia dates from early 5th century and is thought to be the oldest structure in the city. It is built in the form of a Latin cross with a rather striking feature of alabaster windowpanes that give a beautiful soft pearly light. The early mosaics have a remarkable intensity, particularly the predominantly rich cobalt blue and contrasting gold leaf. The most notable in my memory is a pastoral scene showing Christ the Good Shepherd amidst a flock of woolly looking sheep symbolising the souls of the saved in heaven. Once again the colours were brilliant with great vitality and rhythm in the design that is quite breathtaking.

The neighbouring church of San Vitale was so close we had no difficulty in including it in our afternoon's tour. It was built a century later, and here the art of mosaic reached its summit with even richer and more diverse colours. The kaleidoscopic effect is dazzling wherever light touches the irregularities of the thousands of shimmering tesserae, never more so than in the splendid pageantry of the tableaux of Justinian and Theodora. The emperor and empress together with their respective retinues are richly dressed in a splendid illusion of velvets, furs, brocades, and cloth of gold. After the plain brick exterior of the building, this glittering spectacle within is all the more breathtaking. The building takes the form of an octagon, extravagantly pillared and arched in the flowing undulations of the Moorish tradition. The capitals too show the same influence with intricate carvings of exquisite stone lacework, and to complete the overall symmetry the pavement continues the eight-sided form, each section a complex pattern in vari-coloured marbles.

Given particular prominence in the Green Guide, positively not to be missed, is Sant'Apollinare in Classe situated about three miles to the south of Ravenna, but we had reached saturation point and postponed this ultimate revelation to the following day. For the moment, priorities were for food and a bed for the night. Accordingly, the sea being temptingly close and the name Lido di Dante significant on this day, we made that our goal.

The road to the coast cut straight through majestic pine forests, the green shade coming as a soothing and welcome relief after the sun-baked city streets and in less than half an hour we were by the sea. Here at last was that legendary sea, the cradle of our civilisation, and the focal point of our own dreams and expectations. In our hot dusty state, it was a temptation to plunge there and then into those tranquil pearly waters but common sense prevailed, we must first attend to practicalities. Three times, we recited the set piece, 'Ha una camera per favore' only to receive negative responses, but at the fourth a dull little albergo facing inland we were offered a room and thankfully took possession. The proprietress was a real Italian mama figure of enormous girth and she promised us a meal 'piu tarde', which for some reason conjured up a vision of mountains of spaghetti. Still, we had to eat and meanwhile the sea called insistently and we obeyed the call.

In the rapidly failing light, the sea and sky seemed to merge, the whole indefinite space taking an opalescent sheen unbroken by ripple or cloud. It seemed a shame to mar such perfection but we overcame any aesthetic scruples by the time we reached the water's edge. What a perfect way to end this supreme day. I felt I could swim forever in the sublimely warm and apparently endless sea, the ancient trade route between east and west, between the Venetian Empire and the Orient. But then I remembered that I was hungry and La signora was preparing food. So much for the soul of romance.

Supper came as a wonderful surprise. We were not faced with the anticipated pasta but instead feasted on Veneto excellence, a la cucina casalinga, real home cooking. The delicious fish soup was a meal in itself but it was followed by an imaginative risotto made from chicken livers, ham, and parmesan cheese, with a typical Bacchantic bowl of fruit from which to select desert. If this was a foretaste of things to come, we should not complain.

Of the Lido, itself there is not much to say. It was typical of its kind, seemingly built in a hurry without imagination or style, simply to cash in on the age of leisure that brought more and more people to the sea. And that is precisely what it did for us so I should not be too critical.

We left early the next morning; about sevenish if I remember correctly, and although this might seem, an unsocial hour for someone not tied to a precise schedule, we had our ulterior motive. Not being conforming tourists, it has always been our policy to avoid the popular group times, consequently, as we knew that Sant Apollinare would attract crowds we opted to arrive early for the privilege of solitude. What we so missed in recounted legend we gained in the intense personal satisfaction.

The Basilica stands in attractive open countryside, the tall cylindrical campanile being visible for some considerable distance as you approach. The church built from the long flat rose-coloured brick characteristic of Ravenna, looked magnificent in the early morning sun. No wonder it has the reputation of being the most perfect church in Ravenna. It was wonderfully quiet, not a single coach to be seen, and inside, the few other early birds were swallowed up in the immense space. It was difficult to realise that this remarkably well preserved structure dated from 549 AD, its basilica form, shining marble pillars, and airy lightness from generous windows give it an almost contemporary ambience, but there is no mistaking the antiquity of the mosaics.

The apse is most impressive. St. Apollinaris stands erect with upraised arms in the midst of grazing sheep and formalised vegetation, his solemn gaze focused upon the great Latin cross that dominates the gold-starred heavens. The Triumphal arch contains a stylised composition of Christ with twelve lambs that represent the twelve apostles while on pedestals at either side and below stand the Archangels Michael and Gabriel, and St. Mathew and St. Luke. It was a wrench to turn away from this feast of harmonious colour and form and we were certainly glad to have taken the good green book's hint, Sant' Apollinare should certainly not be missed.

Ravenna wore quite a different face this morning when we stopped for breakfast of cappuccino and panini at a cafe in the Piazza del Popolo. It is a fairly intimate square by Italian standards graced by arcades and two interesting 15th century Venetian columns and on this bright morning the multi-coloured sunshades outside the many cafes made of it another sort mosaic. We later shopped for a few supplies along narrow streets where merchandise spilled onto pavements and a bustling atmosphere had ousted yesterday's somnolence. The place swarmed with cyclists who greatly outnumbered cars reminding us of some English University cities. By mid-morning we were away on the road again, still maintaining a southerly trend but without any idea of where we would be at the end of the day.

Nothing noteworthy marked this journey. It was one of many in which the pleasure was derived simply from movement, a positive awareness of living. But the greatest of pleasure can fade with fatigue and there comes a time when it is necessary to stop for shelter and rest. On this occasion the only albergo for miles was obviously favoured by long haul lorry drivers, their great vehicles dwarfing our Fulvia the only motor car in the parking area. We hoped that these giants of the road would not resent our intrusion and went inside to make inquiries. Yes, we could stay, although it seemed that I

47

detected a hint of surprise on the face of the rather dour receptionist.

Supper when it came was a shock, an experience best forgotten; yet its very awfulness is fixed in the memory. It was as far removed from the meal of yesterday as poles asunder, but thankfully, it was an isolated case. Mostly the cucina Italiana was both palatable and nutritious and by and large suited us.

The curtain raiser was a tepid greyish minestra with a flavour to match its appearance. It was served by a gloomy looking waiter who had the audacity to offer second helpings when a blind man could see that we had hardly touched the first. The main course was no better. We were faced with a mess of crunched up chicken, at least we understood it to be chicken, but on dissection it proved to be all grease, skin and bone, and this was garnished with unidentifiable malevolent looking vegetables. The plates were removed without comment and all we could do was to take the edge off our hunger by emptying the customary basket of bread and likewise a couple of bottles of wine. We were forced to conclude that Italian 'camionisti' must be endowed with constitutions of cast-iron to survive on such fare.

We were now somewhere in the gentle landscape of Umbria, and on what promised to be yet another incandescent day of blue and gold we prepared for another departure, another expectant beginning filled as ever with irrepressible avidity to move. Stevenson knew this sensation and summed it up succinctly when he said, 'For my part I travel not to go anywhere, but to go, I travel for travel's sake. The great affair is to move'.

We were now moving into the hills where Francis of Assisi once lived, and where in the year 1214 he founded a monastery at La Verna. In a beautiful isolated spot, we found the monastery perched amongst ancient pines and beeches high on a precipitous chalk cliff. It has always been a popular place for pilgrims and had its share today. We had no choice on this occasion but to join them. In fact the place was very   extensive and easily adsorbed unobtrusively the pilgrims and ourselves. We spent several hours wandering in and out of quiet chapels decorated with the unmistakable blue and white glazed terracottas of Della Robbia. It is an amazing collection covering all aspects of the Christian story from the Nativity to the Crucifixion. A woodland path led to an austere cavern that is reputed to have been the sleeping quarters of the saint, his bed an iron grill placed on a rock shelf, a self imposed penance that typified his vows of extreme poverty. Between times there were endless winding forest paths to follow, shaded by monumental trees, and vantage points giving panoramic views of the countryside below. Our road could be seen snaking away into the distance to disappear in the shimmer of the noonday heat. It was tempting to linger in that arborial haven but our master, the road, called us relentlessly, inspiring our curiosity to top the next rise and reach for the distant horizon.

The afternoon was still and quiet and very hot. We were now deep in the very heart of Italy, travelling through fertile vineyards, peach orchards and wheat fields. On a hill in the centre of this richly fertile plane we came to the old town of Arezzo, built in rising terraces and crowned by a citadel. We stopped for cold drinks and a stretch of the legs and felt something of the historic atmosphere of a town rooted in Etruscan times but this time we had no wish to disturb the deep slumbering siesta and went on to Lake Trasimeno and another hilltop town, Cortona.

The lake was a let down. Any hopes we had fostered of a refreshing bathe in splendid sylvan surroundings were dashed when confronted by acres of unsavoury drought-level mud flats. It was not even possible to find solace in the famous views as the heat-haze restricted visibility making a beige fog of distance. And the final straw came when set upon by mosquitoes as we attempted a lakeside walk. Defeated, we beat a hasty retreat.

Cortona provided a room at the Hotel Nuovo Centrale, which also boasted the luxury of a full-sized bath as part of its private facilities. The usual so far had been a shower, or at best   a hipbath, and my grumbling sciatica craved a good unrestricted wallow. The luxury ended there. Hotel Nuovo Centrale turned out to be the noisiest place in our entire experience making sleep well nigh impossible. As if the extreme heat were not annoyance enough we were treated to what appeared to be a domestic war of attrition. Screams, raised angry voices slamming of doors and staccato running footsteps reverberated through echoing tiled corridors and stairwell for what seemed the entire night. At one point Eric leapt out of bed, stopping only to grab a pair of underpants before bursting out into the corridor with an imperious demand for silence. He had not spent a lifetime schoolmastering for nothing. The effect was miraculous. Warring factions withdrew and an uneasy silence of a fragile cease-fire gave a couple of hours respite.

The peace was short lived but for a different reason. With the dawn, we were awakened by the screech of traffic at the junction traffic lights below our room. It was an unscheduled early departure that morning. The hotel, as with many small establishments, lacked facilities for meals, the custom being to breakfast at one of the many local bars and it was at one of these that we hastily swallowed a coffee and brioche before setting off.

Even at this early hour, it was already hot; we were in for a torrid day. The first part of our route was back towards Lake Trasimeno by way of a plain with grim historic associations. It was the scene of a terrible battle in the year 217 BC when Hannibal put to rout the troops of Consul Flaminius and 16,000 Romans were slaughtered on the field. The nearby hamlets of Sanguineto (bloody) and Ossaia (ossuary) remind one by their names of that sad and awful event.

Assisi was the day's objective, some method having crept into the former indiscriminate shape of our wanderings, but first Perugia lay invitingly in our path. We had become so used to the generally tightly enclosed medieval aspect of Italian towns that we were surprised, and not a little dismayed to run into a straggling area of high-rise modern suburbs. We were not aware of the fact that this was one of Italy's most rapidly expanding urban developments due in part no doubt to the renown of her university.

Leaving the Fulvia to sizzle in a dusty car park in the midst of the unshaded residential sprawl, we approached the ramparts that led into the old centre, the Perugia of our expectations. The contrast between suburb and 'centro storico' was wonderful and Piazza Novembre 4 was a revelation. It was particularly poignant as I was currently reading a strange 19th century novel by Nathaniel Hawthorne called the Marble Faun. In it, there is one crucial scene, which features the Great Fountain with its Pisano sculptures where Miriam and Count Donatello kept their secret tryst. Theirs was a lonely moonlight scenario, impossible to resurrect in full monarchic sun and noisy crowded square, but not only that, there was another vital difference. The two polygonal basins of the Great Fountains are now enclosed by a protective iron railing, necessary no doubt on account of the great antiquity of the sculptures but from an aesthetic point of view it is rather a detraction not an enhancement.

The two principal buildings in the wedge-shaped square, the Priors' Palace and the Cathedral date from the 14th and 15th centuries and are truly majestic edifices, as impressive as any to be found throughout an impressive countrywide architectural heritage. 'Travelling is the ruin of all happiness' said Fanny Burney, for 'There's no looking at a building after seeing Italy, and like many others before us we were fast becoming victims of this sentiment. Amongst groups of vociferous students we cooled off a little, our resting-place the fan-shaped steps leading up to the miniature pink and white marble pulpit from which priors would once have addressed the townsfolk.

Rested, we plunged into the maze of mediaeval streets that follow the contours of the hill. It was rather like circumnavigating a beehive, ruinous to ones sense of direction but profitable in that it revealed countless memorable images. On a mundane level we were also able to replenish food supplies before extricating ourselves from the 'gentle and mystic Umbrian capital' to resume the route to Assisi. The distance was only about 16 miles but it seemed longer in the insuffer-able heat. We felt like Shadrach and Meshach braving the fiery fiery furnace when we climbed aboard Fulvia again. The sleepless night also began to take its toll so that by the time we had reached our target we positively drooped. It was all we could do to drag ourselves from the car to join the throngs patiently footslogging round the famous sights. It was a mis-take to attempt such a project under the circumstances but at the time, it was inconceivable that we should by-pass the notoriously beautiful city.

The actual approach to Assisi is the aspect that I remember most clearly. It appeared in the shimmering heat like an apparition, a majestic pink marble ocean liner sailing across the tawny Umbrian plain, the convent of St. Francis was the prow, the basilica and tiered town, the superstruc-ture while the 14th century fortress tower high on its hilltop made a splendid funnel.

Abandoning the Lancia once again to her fate in an exposed car park, we limped off in search of cooling drinks dreaming of a shady nook, preferably beside a plashing foun-tain. The hope was futile. Crowds packed every available iota of shade. We found some relief in the dark interiors of church-es but were too preoccupied with physical discomfort to appreciate what we were seeing. At last, passing a crowded cafe in the Piazza del Commune, we saw a Chinese couple preparing to vacate the haven of an umbrella shaded table and leapt into their seats with embarrassing haste hardly giv-ing them time to remove themselves. Ordering a large bottle of iced water we settled down for the remainder of the after-noon.

The initial 'mirage' remains perfectly clear in my mind whereas the close quarters of streets, basilicas, monuments etc. have become unfocused dislocated images, a mere hazy memory out of which all you can say is 'Yes I have been to Assisi' Resulting from this experience we temporarily lost the taste for further sightseeing and longed to find a quiet place to hide away until things had simmered down a little.

Late in the afternoon, we drove to Gubbio hoping to find a suitable albergo for the night knowing that Assisi would have been beyond our means even in the unlikely event of finding a vacancy. However, Gubbio was no better. It was both very busy and expensive so there was nothing for it but to move on without an idea of where we could move on to. We followed a road that crossed a mountain range dropping down to the coast close to Fano. By this time we were too late for a room, too late for a meal and absolutely at the end of our tether so the only thing we could do was to find a place to stop the car well away from habitation and shake down for the night. Fortunately we had food aboard emergency rations of tinned sardines, bread (rather well baked by this time) and a bottle of tepid wine. It could have been worse. We were alongside the Adriatic once again but not in a frame of mind to enjoy poetical impulses even with the added incentive of a magnificent starlit night sky. Sleep was all we craved, nothing else mattered and despite the confined conditions, we were quickly out for the count.

At first light, we woke, now more susceptible to our position and an idyllic 'rosy fingered dawn' as we shook off the constraint of sleeping bags to freshen up with a dip in the sea. Nothing stirred either on the shore or the adjacent road so we dispensed with costumes, a wonderfully sensual experience, and no soggy wet suits to deal with afterwards in confined space. We made tea and finished a supply of digestive biscuits carried from home and discussed the situation. An inspired thought emerged from this council. Some years before we had spent a holiday in the Apennines south of Bologna, at a village called Castel d'Aiano, at a high altitude, far enough off the beaten track to ensure a cooler climate and peace and quiet. The 'villeggiatura' were renowned for tranquillity, a word with strong appeal at that particular moment.

At precisely 6 am without another moment's hesitation, we set off northwards for the first time since arriving in Italy. The road was the via Emilia a not very inspiring one but easy driving so early in the day and after a stop for breakfast at eight o'clock, the more interesting ascent of the Apennines took us away from the nondescript trunk road. With ten minutes to spare before lunch we presented ourselves at 'La Lucciola' and what a delightful arrival it was. Maria, wife of the padrone Ariano Righi, the supreme factotum around which La Lucciola revolved, welcomed us with open arms. She remembered our previous visits (twice we had enjoyed her hospitality) and immediately set the wheels in motion to accommodate us sending maids scurrying in all directions, one to set extra plates at table, one to inform the cook, and yet another to prepare a room. Meanwhile, a quick wash-and-brush-up in the cloakroom disguised the worst of our travel-worn aspect, enough to make us presentable at table, and we fell upon the meal as though we had not eaten for a week.

Castel d'Aiano is quite a small community of around 2,000 inhabitants. It is composed of a church, school, post office, a handful of shops, three cafes, a couple of hotels, and an agglomeration of houses, all centred on a sleepy piazza. It is almost entirely contemporary, having been at the heart of bitter fighting during the American army advance of the Second World War. A ferocious bombardment left little of the old village standing and memories of the hardships endured are long and still very much alive. German tourists must obviously be sensitive of this lingering enmity because they are rarely seen in the area, not at this time anyway, whereas in the north, Garda for instance, they outnumbered all other foreign visitors.

We experienced some of this bitterness one day when driving through a neighbouring village. For some reason, the attention of an old man was riveted on our dear Fulvia in an obviously unfriendly manner, if his scowl and clenched gesticulating fist were any indication of his sentiments. Mystified, we stopped and received a volley of language that did not have the stamp of the drawing room in it and at the same time, he continued to shake a defamatory knarled fist at the car. It was a three legs of Man symbol that featured on the nationality plate that had roused the old man to anger. He had, quite understandably, mistaken it for a swastika and us for Germans and when we explained our origins his anger dissolved, he laughed uproariously and shook our hands vigorously, quite reluctant to let us go. We were relieved not to be the true object of such virulent animosity and very sad that it existed at all.

Ariano Righi, our padrone, was always eager to show English visitors a framed picture of honours awarded by the Americans for his part in resistance work during the occupation. It hung in a prominent position in the bar, in spite of the interval of almost forty years that had passed since those violent times.

Sunday in the village was a real holiday; an action packed day when the weekly market transformed the square into the commercial and social event of the week. From a sleepy backwater, it changed overnight into a lively metropolis and the three cafes did a roaring trade. At one the men gathered where all was clamorous debate over endless card games, the second was favoured by the family groups while the teenage fraternity monopolised the other. At one end of the square, a flignt of wide shallow steps led up to the church and even here commerce rubbed shoulders with Sabbath day observance as stall holders utilised the steps while a steady stream of worshippers passed to and fro. Mass said, the church-goers joined in the fray, trying on new shoes on sacred steps or choosing pots and pans or whatever dressed in their Sunday best.

As onlookers, we found it all highly entertaining, and the down-to-earth attitude to religion quite refreshing. There followed another ceremony that was equally entertaining, La Lucciola's Sunday lunch, the culinary high spot of the week. On this day la signora always excelled from the delicious lasagna for primo piatto to the savoury roast chicken aromatic with herbs and garnished with the freshest of vegetables to the pudding, a sweet pastry and ice cream. Simple though it may sound the Italian cook has the knack of transforming the ordinary, with a loving touch, into the realms of 'haute cuisine' To add to the festive spirit of that day every guest received a glass of champagne to drink the health of one who was celebrating a 'name' or saint's day, a custom that was widely practised in the country hotels. The benefactor happened to be our neighbours at table, a retired couple on holiday from Bologna called Dino and Olga Fachinetti. Olga had been a schoolteacher and as such was able to appreciate the difficulties involved with learning and practising a new language. Her patience and encouragement broke down bashful reserve making communication possible and fun. Dino's method wasn't bad either; a liberating extra glass of wine does wonders for the confidence.

It was all so pleasant that we talked about the idea of wintering in the area and looked into the possibility of renting property. Maria nipped that plan in the bud when she reminded us of the severity of winter at this altitude, it was quite usual for snow to lie for weeks at a time. The original intention of finding a temperate niche made more sense and Maria suggested Liguria. 'It is more beautiful with clima mite and caldo' she told us, advice that was to stand us in good stead later.

Restored and recharged once again we made plans for the next exploratory foray into unfamiliar territory. Five days of tranquillity had wiped all pain and discomfort from our minds and we were impatient for action. On August 26th after an emotional leave taking we resumed the journey.

The Mezzogiorno was the objective and in particular, the Gargano Massif, the jutting spur above the 'heel' of Apulia. We had read fascinating accounts describing the region as a natural wilderness, unexploited and unspoilt. Could this be true? Would we be in time? There was a considerable quantity of spade-work to be done before reaching that visionary promised land consisting of a long boring slog back along the Via Emilia, first eastward and then south down the Adriatic coast. Much of this once glorious seaboard with its miles of fine sandy beaches has suffered the fate of so much of the Mediterranean coast, over exploitation. What should have been a joy was a depressing prospect of untidy camp sites or multi storey concrete abominations and litter everywhere. Beaches roadside, pine woods, all desecrated by post-picnic trash that would have been so easy for the individual to take away, (they had presumably been strong enough to carry full cans and food containers) Now it was left to overstretched officials who were obviously fighting a losing battle to maintain their beauty spots.

An overnight stop at Roseto degli Abruzzi was notable only for the first, and last, stomach disorder of the whole of our travels. Eric was taken with a sharp, but fortunately short, attack of sickness and diarrhoea, which nevertheless left him feeling below par for most of the following day. The first part of the journey through Pescara and Termoli was largely unremarkable, a case of the mixture as before, but at last, just before San Severo our road left the Via Emilia and we were off the beaten track. A wonderful deserted landscape fell away in endless undulations of hill and valley, craggy hills spiked with grey limestone and ancient olive trees. These were not the ordered groves of tamed trees seen further north but wild unpruned ancient looking specimens, ungainly and yet graceful at the same time. To see a stirring of air turn the grey-green leaves into a shivering silver cloud is an unforgettable sight, one that never fails to enchant me however many times it is repeated. And yet this same enchantment stems from the most knarled misshapen trunks imaginable, one of nature's bizarre juxtapositions. It could also be said that the olive is something of a life support machine, or has been throughout its long history. It yields oil for cooking and condiment and lighting, oil for cosmetic and medicinal use, not to mention the whole fruit either green or black that when pickled can be used in so many different ways, eaten alone or in cooking. It is hardly surprising that it has been so exalted and that its branches should represent the symbol of peace.

The road was wonderfully quiet, quite a rare phenomenon in Italy, and the infrequent signs of habitation we came across appeared to be deserted. One hilltop village seemed totally abandoned even though there were new buildings or partly built ones, there was not a sign of life. Was it bewitched or stricken by some abominable pestilence as in Greco-Roman times? It was an enigma for which nobody was able to furnish an explanation.

57

After many miles of this depopulated wilderness, we were rudely precipitated back to reality and a raw new road glaringly flanked by the brashest of brash hoardings, not to mention heaps of builder's rubble. The hoardings were selling hotel space, an ominous foreboding of what we might expect when we reached the coast and civilisation. Where was the once innate sense of style in this nation known as 'the mother of the arts'?

Rodi Garganico's shutters came clattering down the minute we entered the town. Narrow roads were jammed with home-bound Lambrettas, Vespas and battered but nimble three-wheeled Piaggios, an odd little vehicle that could go anywhere, from farms, the wildest of mountain tracks and city streets. It was the mule, or beast of burden of the internal combustion engine. This was the lunch-time shut down when the entire population had but one thought in mind, the important focal point of their day, an unrushed convivial family lunch gathering. No use going any further into the town at closing time, and as there was enough food on board for a picnic lunch, we followed directions to the shore.

It was a dream of a beach, one to write home about, sparsely populated golden sands fringing clear aquamarine water and not a scrap of litter to be seen. We could hardly believe our eyes. And the shore road looked good too, not a single high-rise in sight, only an isolated sugar-cube building, bright white with green painted balconies and shutters, and a single-track railway-line that ran alongside the road. So it really was true that a few undeveloped corners could still be found, but for how long we wondered.

Before one could say Giuseppe Verdi we were out of the car and had set up a base camp on the beach, changed into swimsuits and plunged into the sea. The word pollution was not quite so prevalent in the early 80's and we still had faith in the remedial power of sea bathing, it was balm to the body and psyche. While drying off and eating a lunch of melon and prosciutto (wafer thin raw ham) washed down with a light wine drunk from plastic cups, we reviewed the situation and decided to drop anchor if possible here in Rodi. From the beach we could see the town perched upon a jutting headland, it looked alluring and together with the copybook beach persuaded us to stay.

One of the green painted shutters of the square white building carried a 'To Let' sign. Crossing road and railway, the latter by way of a white wooden gate with a simple request to be careful of the trains, we went over to investigate. A courtyard blazed with bougainvillaea, jasmine and huge scarlet geraniums, and there beneath the shade of a pergola a youngish woman sat gossiping with an aged couple. She was quick to respond to our enquiry and we found ourselves ushered into a cool first-floor apartment with a great deal of si si si-ing, and reiterated bellisimos. It was all so quick that we had parted with the equivalent of one hundred pounds for a week's rent before having time to think, but in the euphoria of the moment I suspect that we would willingly have paid more. It was worth a lot for the pleasure of being independent of hotels, and from the trouble of end of day searches for a roof and a bed. We could now eat what we liked and when we liked, deal with a backlog of laundry, and write essential letters. It was even at the back of our minds to come to some arrangement regarding more permanent accommodation.

The Fulvia seemed almost to purr with pleasurable relief when we finally unloaded her, and springs that had for so long borne the brunt of the excessively heavy load returned to normal. This had not been possible before because of space limitations, we were carrying an exorbitant quantity of stuff, and I marvel now when I recall that diminutive sports car's capabilities. The entire kit and caboodle was swallowed with ease, and it and us kept constantly on the move.

Late in the afternoon, a knock on the door woke us from a much-needed siesta. It was the husband of the signora with whom we had arranged the tenancy, our proprietor in fact who had been away teaching English at a local school when we had arrived. He introduced himself in the usual Italian manner, surname first, D'Erico Franco and then to our surprise presented us with a crate of bottled water. This was explained when he warned us that the tap water was not safe,

'It is undrinkable and will give you sickness' he said. Luckily, we had not used any, and although forewarned of the danger of impure water in the remoter districts, the problem had not yet arisen and we neglected to be on our guard. It is quite possible that Eric's indisposition of the night before could have been the result of bad water. He'd had ice cream for desert (I hadn't) and the hotel was not a million miles from Rodi. We thanked Franco for his warning and for the ample supply of a cumbersome necessity.

Franco was a small dapper man of slight build and great energy. Both his movements and speech were quick with no trace of southern languor, and although he spoke to us in English, the force of his torrents of words made his conversation almost incomprehensible. It would have been easier to communicate had he spoken slowly in Italian, however his affability and desire to please overcame all difficulties and he proved to be the most cordial of hosts.

The flat was adequate though not without its faults, the worst being the primitive drainage. The sink blocked on a regular basis and so too did the shower where the water had a tendency to flow across the hall and into the living room rather than through the proper channel. We were thankful for marble tiled floors on such occasions; carpets would have presented serious problems. The kitchen was a rudimentary alcove with the basic cooking equipment of twin calor gas rings, no oven or grill. This was where the art of all-in-the-pot cuisine came into its own; a method still widely used where fuel is both expensive and in short supply. The rest of the flat was roomy and cool, and the balcony with its glorious view more than compensated for the defects: the tiered town on its rocky promontory to the left, the shimmering blue sea on our doorstep, and to the right the road to Vieste and the accompanying railway line backed by low olive covered hills.

Old Rodi was reached by following the coast for about a mile, a pleasant daily constitutional, and then ascending steeply by a series of hairpin bends to a palm-shaded piazza, the social hub of the community. A few shops and cafes opened onto the square in which permanent traffic chaos reigned, the norm apparently in a rural society that had not yet learned the code or discipline of the road. Everyone claimed the right of way and this was not improved by the knots of vociferous idlers who stood around in-groups impervious to the chaos around them. These appeared to be mainly men, the senior citizen fraternity with time on their hands. The old women congregated close to their homes keeping a watchful eye on small children while endlessly knitting or making lace, their hands were rarely unoccupied.

Another shorter way up into the town was by way of steeply stepped streets and alleyways. It was always reverberatingly noisy, the open doors and windows offering glimpses of domestic life that could hardly have altered since the dwellings were first built early last century. There was one radical difference. The women's gossip carried on from balcony to balcony could never be described as 'sotto voce' but now it had to compete with the collective sounds of television. Every home, however humble, seemed to have one and regardless of whether anyone was actually viewing they were left on, a constant jingle of pop music, or declamatory speech, or idiot laughter, incongruous in such surroundings. We watched a young girl come from one of the houses carrying a tray of prepared pizza, and following her for some distance up into the town, saw her take it into the communal bakery. This was a reminder that we were not alone in being ovenless, which seemed illogical in view of the ubiquitous television, a strange priority to my mind.

Aesthetically the town had little to offer, the distant view being its greatest asset. From the coast road, it was an impressive unit of warm buff-coloured stone occupying a rugged outcrop of rock that protruded island-like into the sea. Giant palms and cascading bougainvillea gave grace and colour to the prospect but otherwise, there was no more to it. At close quarters, not only were the individual buildings lacking in interest but there was also a foul smell of bad drainage. Previous thoughts of making a protracted stay in Rodi quickly evaporated on close acquaintance.

It became obvious that isolation in such a place was pure fantasy and completely impractical. With few books, only sketchy knowledge of the language, a radio that was virtually useless and no city amenities at all to fall back on, the winter months would be impossible. We needed the proximity of some great cultural centre with galleries and concerts to supplement our own meagre resources. One useful piece of information that was to prove invaluable was given to us in a casual conversation on the beach one-day. A family from the city of Vicenza in the north were holidaying in an adjacent apartment and had brought their radio with them, but it was not the usual strident clamour one over-hears in public places but real music. We were so intrigued we just had to ask them what it was, and learned that it was the Italian equivalent of BBC Radio 3, consequently after a few minutes of patient knob twiddling we had a usable radio.

Meanwhile, la dolce vita at the D'Errico apartment raced past, and conscious as we were that this respite could only last a short time we wallowed in it, not venturing any further into the peninsula. This omission was very much regretted when it was too late to do anything about it, and it was not the only missed opportunity. The excessive heat that induced ennui was our excuse. It was necessary to pace oneself. One of the many advantages of the free nomadic life we had chosen to live was being cut off from all forms of 'news', the gloom and doom of media stresses. We felt inviolate in a cocoon of oblivion that left our thoughts free to enjoy the moment, the here and now.

As August drifted into September, we took long walks, swam twice a day and enjoyed wonderful aperitif times watching the sunset from the balcony. There is something very special about sunset over water be it lake or sea. Anticipation mounts as the sun drops and all at once creates a glorious molten path of gold, so bright as to be almost painful to look upon, yet so brief that one is loth to look away. Often at dusk the D'Errico's would invite us to join them on the terrace, when friends or sundry relatives might drop in to join Franco and his wife and children and the old couple who were Signora D'Errico's parents. There might be an occasional hand of cards but the more usual pastime was talking. We did not doubt the warmth of our welcome despite being unable to understand a word of their rapid patois, except for the old man's reiterated international query: 'tut' OK '? Nevertheless, it was evident from smiles and nods that the family took great pride in Franco's ability to speak with the 'stranieri' while we the foreigners felt privileged to be admitted to their circle.

Our diet underwent a radical change during this period that has never been reversed. It began as an experiment with what at first seemed quite meagre raw materials but culminated in some very successful concoctions. The poor cooking facilities plus the expense of meat meant finding alternatives, it was simply a case of 'necessity being the mother of invention'. There was no shortage of good fresh vegetables, and with pasta, rice, chicken and fish, plus a dash of ingenuity, a new and healthy diet evolved that has been maintained ever since. I learned some of the Italian's ways with sauces many of which are based on the humble tomato and this reminds me of an amusing incident that occurred at the house of D'Errico.

I had been shopping and was almost home when I realised that I had forgotten to buy tomatoes. Annoyed but reluctant to trek all the way back again, I turned into the courtyard and stopped short in amazement. At the foot of the steps that led to our apartment was the greatest quantity of tomatoes I had ever seen; an immense mound of shiny, ripe, scarlet, fruit. Was this the work of the Gods? Had they taken pity on my forgetfulness? If so this was taking things a bit too far, a kilo was all I needed, this was ridiculous. As it turned out, the explanation involved no divine intervention on my behalf. It appeared that Franco had a brother who ran a small farm on which he grew tomatoes and also oranges and in return for help at harvest time, the family received a share of these crops. As Signora D'Errico dryly explained 'Tutti gli italiani piaciono spaghetti, e spaghetti a bisogna di pomodori'. This tomato mountain was their winter's supply of sauce and it took two days of labour over charcoal and wood burning braziers for the women to cook and bottle it all.

The week drew to a close and it was with mixed feelings that we made preparations to move on. Franco made us an offer of two or three days more free of charge, - it was the end of the season and no more visitors were expected - and we were almost tempted to accept but for that sense of change in the air that summer's end portends. There was still so much to see before the need to settle somewhere before the winter curtailed our movements. With some regrets but exhilarated by anticipation we said goodbye on Friday the 3rd of September and with promises to return sometime in the future, left Rodi Garganico for the western shore.

Chapter Five

From Darkness into Light

'Between the idea and the reality, between the motion and the act, falls the shadow'.

T.S.Eliot.

With the change in direction came a subtle alteration in attitude. The wanderlust was almost satiated and although reluctant to admit the change even to each other, we began to crave stability. Common sense undermined our resolve to achieve a different, perhaps an outlandish way of living, but we did not give way without a struggle. The journey this far had revealed nothing positive in the way of a permanent abode to suit all stipulations; a benign climate, attractive environs, and stimulating cultural amenities within easy reach, all at a cost that came within our limited budget. But we were still optimistic; all that was needed was diligent action and a little less vacillation. Maria Righi's advice shone like a beacon before us as we pinned our faith more and more in the potentialities of either Tuscany or Liguria.

From the Gargano spur, we crossed the 'leg' of the Italian mainland in the direction of Campania with the intention while in the vicinity of visiting Pompeii. The road meandered over harvested wheatlands now bare of even stubble, the freshly ploughed furrows creating a fascinating study in light and shade. Varicoloured earth made a patchwork of terracotta, dun, tawny and umber that was broken by the occasional vertical line of a lone umbrella pine or a straggly eucalyptus that served to underline the emptiness of the landscape. The temperature soared again once we were away from the freshening influence of the sea, and as on many a similar journey the important concern around mid-day was to find shade for a lunch break. True to form the search was a long and apparently hopeless one so that when at last we came upon a derelict farm and a few impoverished shrubby trees, we reacted as though it were paradise itself. There was the fig tree loaded with ripe fruit and even an ancient apple tree that despite its lichen covered trunk had managed to bear a number of sound and deliciously sweet apples. This was one of our luckier breaks. Sheltering in the valuable shade of a crumbling stone wall we dined serenaded by the dreamy whirring hum of a thousand winged insects and sharp stridulations of cicadas. It was a perfect place for a siesta, soporific sounds, the heat and effects of tepid wine were hardly conducive to action and it took considerable will power to tear ourselves away onto the road again.

The bare agricultural lands of the interior dropped behind as the road began the tortuous climb over the backbone of the southern Apennines, an area that had apparently suffered severely from excessive drought conditions during July and August. The formerly lush wooded slopes were now reduced to forests of skeletal charcoal stumps following devastating fires. It seemed impossible that these mutilated hills could ever recover.

But worse was to come. Some distance beyond the ravaged forests, we came upon villages giving an impression of never having recovered from wartime sieges. Signs of severe bombardment hastily patched up, heaps of rubble, gaping roofs and precarious walls, and a bone-shaking road surface had us completely mystified. When we reached Mercato san Severino and saw its ruined church, the awful truth dawned. This was the aftermath of the 1981 earthquake that left a trail of death and destruction over a wide area of the region and this same church must have been the scene of tragedy in which almost an entire village community lost their lives. Driven from their quaking homes they looked for safety in the church that they believed invincible but the roof caved in killing all who had taken shelter. A solitary chandelier still dangled precariously from a surviving timber, pitiable memorial of the catastrophe.

A few half-hearted signs of repair could be seen but most of the houses looked abandoned, only waiting for the bulldozer to finish them off altogether. A few caravans and temporary huts emphasised the realities of such disasters, a third winter loomed ahead, harsh and uncompromising at this altitude, and this was to be endured in these inadequate and fragile shelters.

The pathos of such sights, and there were many, trimmed our own problems down to size and the hazards of driving over violently distorted roads were endured with rather more resignation that we would otherwise have done. Gaps cracks, and potholes were commonplace and in many places only half the original width remained, a ragged shelf left clinging to a mountainside with the rest forming a pre-cipitous avalanche of broken tarmacadam and rubble. It was heart-in-the-mouth- stuff with hardly any margin of error and we were reminded of the extent of the problems that must have faced relief workers after the calamity. There was criti-cism at the time for what seemed lamentable lack of speed and organisation in mounting rescue operations, and this ter-rifying journey left us in no doubt as to the enormity of their task; the difficult terrain, vast distances involved and the breakdown in communications. Many stricken villages involved were perched on craggy hilltops, difficult of access even at the best of times.

We were unusually silent as we grappled with the twisting descent down to the coast in the region of Salerno, shaken both mentally and physically by this manifestation of nature tyrannical. To shake off the melancholy state of mind we tried the antidote of beauty, the legendary Costa Amalfitana, but it was a mistake. The busy corniche demands absolute concentration at all times, it is not a road to be rec-ommended at the end of an exhausting day, consequently its scenic splendour failed to extract from us the appreciation it deserved.

We called a halt at Maiori at the very end of our teth-er, booked a room for the night and breathed great sighs of relief as we shook off the dust of the road. Half and hour later we had recovered sufficiently to join the ever recurring quest for a place to eat and were rewarded with the discovery of Trattoria Mario and Maria. It was a pretty vinehung pavement café, all crisp gingham and colourful potted plants, quiet enough to be restful without being dead, perfect in fact for our convalescent need. A corner table gave seclusion without exclusion and with an excellent pasta meal, speciality of Signor Mario, washed down by an equally excellent wine, equilibrium was gradually restored. Satisfying hunger and thirst following an active though abstemious day must surely be one of life's greatest pleasures, and when such satisfaction takes place in such a salubrious environment the memory is long cherished.

The following morning revealed the full glory of that magnificent coast. Enchantment lay round every bend in the tortuous road and as we now drove on the seaward side we could appreciate the full drama of its situation above and at the extreme edge of vertically plunging cliffs that dropped sheer into the bluest of blue seas. We skirted deep gorges that alternated with reefs topped by Saracen towers, crawled slowly through busy villages of white houses that seemed to cascade like avalanches towards the sea, and everywhere there was blossom and lush greenery. We turned inland at Vietri towards Pompeii believing that we were turning away from the spectacular, but the fantastic landscapes did not end there, the vistas continued to thrill.

Pompeii was a deeply moving experience. True to our ideal form, we arrived as the gates were opened and for the first hour or so had the place virtually to ourselves. Conditions were near perfect as we walked amongst the noble ruins, the deep silence broken by only our own footfalls and the occasional call of birds. The sky was cloudless, like an inverted Wedgwood bowl [in the shimmering distance by] a lilac coloured mountain range dominated by Vesuvius. It was odd to think that by its very act of destruction the volcano was responsible for preserving for posterity the one-time sumptuous Roman City.

The splendid isolation could not last of course and the magic faded as the crowds grew. The Temple of Jupiter with its flanking arches of Caligula and Nero lost the sense of Roman presence and timelessness under the impact of the 20th century camera-clicking invasion. But it was the increasing heat, not so much the crowds that made us decide to move on. There was every indication that we were in for another inexorable day so we left Pompeii's stones sweltering beneath a fitting monarchic sun. Successfully evading the inevitable overtures of insistent souvenir sellers now massed outside the gates, we made our getaway.

The remainder of the early September day was horrendous, possibly the worst in many respects of all the journeys we made. The sun shone with an unrelenting brassy glare that paralysed the senses and impaired judgement, to such an outrageous degree that instead of reducing the scheduled mileage it was actually increased. On and on we pressed, impotent to terminate the gruelling torment. We even resorted to motorway in the mistaken belief that brisker pace would result in cooler air currents but there seemed to be little air about that day, at any rate there was no relief to be found.

Towards 6 o'clock, Tivoli came up on the signboards and we made a bid to escape from the treadmill. Memories of Villa d'Este's cascades and fountains beckoned like a desert mirage, but it was only a mirage. The gardens were closed for the day and exhaustive efforts to find a bed for the night proved abortive forcing us back onto the road with the resignation of despair. We felt condemned to drive forever on a journey through hell.

With the demise of the sun and ensuing darkness some reasoning power was restored, enough anyway to pick out the town of Riete from the map in the fervent hope that there we would find food and shelter. At last, the agony came to an end with a room and a meal at Albergo Italia. The receptionist must have had her doubts when two such disreputable characters as we presented had the audacity to enter her shinning marble hall but she was magnanimous. The rest of that day is completely blank, I think I must have been asleep on my feet.

The following day was Sunday and as different from its predecessor as chalk from cheese. The air sparkled with an unbelievable freshness hardly visualised as ever being possible during yesterday's infernal drive. Riete lies in the geographical centre of Italy, a meeting point of valleys that form a cultivated basin of lush meadows and shady beechwoods. This smiling Riete basin reminded me of certain words from the Odyssey where 'Vegetable beds of various kinds are neatly laid out row upon row, and making a smiling patch of never failing green'.

Somewhere along the road to Terni we digressed from the direct route in order to look for a waterfall known as the Cascata delle Marmore (Marble Water-fall) so called because of 3 consecutive marble clefts that form the impressive 600 foot cascade. Rainbows of bouncing spray at the various levels create a vision of loveliness by which we lingered for some time enjoying the cooling sight and sound of the spectacle. Back on the route, our road followed yet another corniche, this one overlooking the Velino Gorges and giving extensive views of hilltop villages and frequent tantalising glimpses of a distant lake. But from the floor of the valley, clouds of acrid smoke and fumes settled like a giant mushroom in the inert air, and as we came closer we could discern a vast agglomeration of cooling towers, factory chimneys, and general industrial accoutrements belonging to the electrical generating industry. This source of power supplied a considerable area including Rome itself.

We came to the distinguished small city of Todi, a charming town noted for its three sets of walls, Etruscan, Roman, and Medieval, and a pleasant situation on the banks of the Tiber. We stopped for a short walk along some of the peaceful old streets with their rich diversity of buildings, Romanesque Gothic and Renaissance all living happily together, an architectural student's dream. The air vibrated with the sound of church bells, and people strolled about the streets and squares dressed in their Sunday best intent on

enjoying themselves. It had every indication of a holiday, perhaps even a special 'festa', but we were not to know for we
were travelling on.

Later, at the centre of Ficolle, a straggling nondescript
place, we were stopped by the police. Our initial reaction
when faced by uniformed officialdom was illogically, one of
guilt. What have we done wrong, or worse still, of what crime
suspected. Then reason returned perhaps an accident ahead
or the road has disappeared in an avalanche. The trouble
was, our young carabiniere could not make us understand
the local dialect or patois defeated us and we were brusquely
waved aside to be ignored once out of circulation. Having
done his duty our interlocutor quickly rejoined his cronies at
an adjacent café-bar, meanwhile knots of people stood as
though waiting for something to happen, but what?

As time passed, we became more and more exasperat-
ed by the unexplained delay, and we made another attempt to
extract an explanation from the policeman and it was then
that a bystander cleared the enveloping fog. Two simple words
explained all, corsa bicicletta. All that frustration and needless worry for the sake of a local bike race that was due at
some unspecified time to pass through the town.

We saw the funny side of the situation, the tinpot
drama, and settled down to wait for the great event. Leaving
the official party in command at their café, we found another
quieter bar and ordered ham rolls and beer to help pass the
time. There was nothing behind the town; it was just one long
mediocre street with nothing to offer the sightseer, so beer
and ham rolls it had to be. And at last, something in the attitude of the bystanders communicated the imminent
approach of the racing cyclists. First on the scene was the
entourage, a nose to tail procession of team support cars and
motorbikes, with blaring horns, revving engines and a deaf-
ening amplified commentary that shattered the drowsy
Sunday peace. This must be an important race we told ourselves, suitably impressed. And then a lone rider appeared
pedalling furiously to the encouraging shouts and applause of
the crowd. He must be a local hero, but he passed so quickly

that it all seemed a bit of an anticlimax after the frenetic build up. However, the big scene was yet to come with the arrival only seconds later of the chasing bunch, a turbulent stream of rainbow-jerseyed super men in hot pursuit of the hare who had managed to make a lone break from their ranks. It was an impressive rush of jostling elbowing riders jockeying for a dominant position. We cheered them on their way and were then, allowed to continue on ours, which happened to be the road to Sienna.

How different two consecutive days can be from each other, the one when nothing seems to go right, and the next a sequence of interest packed hours. On the first the day drags one down while the second stimulates and uplifts, filling one with joie de vivre. This weekend was a typical example. The heat was not oppressive, the route interesting without being too demanding, and now we had Sienna to explore and from the moment we left the car and walked beneath the battlemented Porta Romana we felt that this beautiful Gothic city was there purely for our entertainment.

Being Sunday, the public buildings were closed but it didn't matter a bit, two hours passed like a dream. We paced the Piazza del Campo lost in a reverie of ghostly cheering crowds and panting horses, the overwhelming excitement of medieval costumed Palio delle Contrade. In fact the present emptiness of the scallop-shaped piazza was to our advantage as it left plenty of room to stand back and admire one of Italy's finest public buildings, the Palazzo Pubblico, The Torre del Mangia, so named after a bellringer of the Middle Ages, is the tallest in Italy at 286 ft, fifty feet higher than the great Bell Harry Tower of Canterbury. The duomo's magnificent wedding cake architecture showed up to perfection lit by the afternoon sun against a cobalt blue September sky. This was one building remaining open on Sunday giving us the opportunity to view its dramatic interior of alternating bands of black and white marble. The effect is quite dazzling. It would be impossible to describe in detail the work of artists too numerous to imagine, the architects, and sculptors, the entire edifice is a complete work of art including the marble paving designed by a group of the most eminent artists of the Renaissance.

After this, we wandered away from the beaten track and the notable sights to poke about in our usual perverse manner down lesser streets to be rewarded by a lucky encounter. A small group of alfieri (flag throwers) arrestingly costumed in black and white, paraded in the swaggering style that medieval costume seems to demand. They flung their banners high in the air and caught them again with consummate ease in time to the blood-stirrring beat of drums. It was a delightful cameo of what the great palio festival would be like.

Back in Piazza del Campo, it was time to rest the aching feet and take some refreshment before resuming the final stage of the day's journey. We ordered tea at a café close by the flag seller's stalls and for once I was nearly tempted by the gorgeous silks, replicas of the contrade banners, that were for sale as souvenirs. The multi-colours clustered together and fluttering in the breeze made an eye-catching display. With our tea, we tried a slice of the famous sienna cake or panforte, a nougat-like mixture of roasted nuts, candied peel and spices, delicious but not to be recommended to anyone with suspect fillings.

The time was approaching when we could reasonably expect to find, or at least start looking for, a place to live. Lucca was top of the list and was not far away and though reluctant to turn our backs on the seductions of sienna, the excitement of house hunting drew us away. Lucca would be easily reached by the following day if we could cover a few more intervening kilometres before stopping for the night. We drove through a place with the remarkable name of Poggibonsi that must surely have been the birthplace of Billy Bunter, but amusing though its name may sound it offered nothing in visual attraction being a starkly modern industrial centre.

When we reached Montespertoli there was no question of going further for we ran into chaotic traffic that more or less decided for us that this must be the end of the road for the day. The place looked in celebratory mood with bright bunting and stalls and merry-go-rounds, and we hoped sincerely that the holiday crowd was local otherwise our chances of finding a room would be dashed. With relief we found our hopes to be justified and obtained a room at the very first attempt. The proprietor obviously knew that the revels would go on into the night and thoughtfully suggested that we might prefer a room at the back well away from the noisy square. His consideration was greatly appreciated later when the fiesta really began to warm up.

Our own day ended in festive mood at a nearby pizzeria. The place was full of family parties celebrating the fiesta and there was nothing reticent in their enjoyment, conversations were held at full throttle and the air pulsated with good humour. Things almost got out of hand when a bat flew in through an open window. Its radar system must have misfired, anyway it was an unwelcome guest at the party and was chivvied from table to table by feminine screams and masculine threats until it found an escape route and the party simmered down again.

During the night we had the first real rain since leaving Lake Iseo, a prolonged and heavy downpour that left a lot of water on the road when we started out in the morning. Although it had laid the dust, the air was still sultry and even more enervating than the direct sun's heat had been. We were quite glad to have only a moderate mileage planned and were looking forward to the prospect of this being the final stage of our peregrinations.

We quickly covered the short distance into Lucca and with hopes high began quartering the town in search of estate agents. It is a compact walled town built on the plan of a Roman military camp, nevertheless there was a great deal of ground to cover in the incredible maze of narrow streets. We found plenty of agents but none that dealt with rented property. Each enquiry was received with nonchalance and abrupt negatives but we kept going, sure that somewhere we would stumble on a man of sympathy who knew of just such an apartment that would suit us. But it was all to no avail and the only advice extracted was to try Viareggio, the coastal holiday resort with plenty of winter lets to be had. This was not exactly what we had in mind when planning to live in the Italian style and consequently pride and enthusiasm were both a little dented.

We retreated to a vantage point on the tree-lined ramparts, one of the great attractions of the town, and reviewed the situation. It was ironical to find ourselves looking down on an exquisite garden, the very epitome of what one expects of an Italian garden; an octagonal green pool and fountain at the centre, beds of scarlet salvias and geraniums, and avenues flanked by classical statues. It was the sum of my dreams and here they were sliding inexorably beyond reach, but no, I would not give up hope, we had come too far to throw in the towel so easily.

However, there was nothing further to be done here, the siesta hour was upon us and all offices closed until evening, which left us with the usual problem of where to stay that night. Half-heartedly flipping through the Red Michelin accommodation guide my interest rallied when I spotted an entry that read: Hotel Villa Casanova. 16th century mansion set in a wooded valley, with extensive gardens, swimming pool, 1:2 kms from Lucca. The description was too idyllic for the modest rating; there must be some mistake I thought while at the same time clinging to the fantasy of sleeping in a 16th century mansion. It could not do any harm to at least look at the place we decided, with swimming pool and gardens and wooded valleys dangling like carrots in front of our jaded eyes.

Not anticipating any problem in locating the villa in such a small town, we began by circumnavigating the ramparts, keeping a weather eye open for the typical hotel signpost. We soon found what we were looking for and confidently followed the direction, or what seemed to be the direction, but something was radically wrong. The Villa Casanova failed to materialise and we arrived back at the starting point wondering if this was somebody's idea of a joke. Another attempt was more successful with the discovery of a second sign practically obscured by foliage, and away we sailed on the trail again.

We were not out of the wood yet. Miles ticked by and yet on enquiring at a filling station we learned that the direction was correct and with still some distance to go. It became obvious eventually that the estimated distance should have read twelve kms. The discrepancy being a simple decimal point error. In due course, after winding through undulating wooded countryside, a valley opened and revealed the elusive villa. Michelin's decimals may have been at fault but their description lacked nothing, it was everything we could have wished down to an oleander-shaded garden, the very incarnation of our dreams.

With a sense of being removed from reality, we found the price to be well within our prescribed budget and rooms to spare. It must be an illusion, a figment of our overstretched imagination, yet as we followed the young, and quite substantial receptionist, we felt the she was definitely of this world, there was nothing remotely ethereal about her. We were led across the gracious entrance hall and up a sweeping staircase to inspect the first of a choice of rooms. What we saw almost defies description. A massive door opened onto an enormous dormitory. The atmosphere was musty as though from long disuse and though shuttered there was sufficient light filtering through the slats to disclose three matrimoniale. I should explain for the benefit if the uninitiated that Italian beds are about half as wide again as an English King size and here there were three. But that was not all. The room was also furnished with wardrobes, dressing tables, chests and armchairs all of equally gargantuan dimension.

Maintaining tremendous self-control, we asked to see the second room fearing the worst but hoping for the best, that is, a little moderation. We were led back to the ground floor and a room directly off the entrance hall. It was still what you might describe as a baronial chamber but at least within the feasible. With the heavy shutters flung back, the lofty white-walled room flooded with sunlight and we proceeded to act the part and make ourselves at home. First a shower in the palatial bathroom – all heavy white porcelain and gleaming brass- then tea in the solitary splendour in the great hall by which time we had begun to enjoy ourselves and unwind, the disappointment of the morning fading into insignificance.

Relaxed and refreshed there was now time to take a closer look at this wonderful residence and it was soon apparent that for all its grandeur there was an element of gentle deterioration and neglect that suggested the dissipation of former fortunes. The signs of past splendour could be seen everywhere but mostly reduced and a little frayed at the edges. The pictures were mainly old oils of the family portrait category, gilt-framed mirrors were tarnished and flyblown, and the few once handsome urns and vases were now crazed and chipped. The furniture like that of the bedrooms already described was large and opulent but uncomfortable and so faded that it was impossible to say what the original patterns and colours had been. But the fabric of the building still retained the magnificence of 16-century craftsmanship in its masonry, woodwork, marble and plasterwork.

One unusual object that could scarcely ever have been considered as ornamental was a huge iron cauldron that dominated the entrance hall. It must have measured four foot both in height and diameter, quite large enough to supply an army with a hot meal. It made one think of cannibals and witches. We wondered how it was ever moved, either for use or simply to its present position.

The garden was lovely. It too was neglected but still maintained the charm of good design that has benefited by maturity. It was sweet with the scent of full-blown roses, with jasmine and carnations. Tall trees shaded a wide terrace bounded by stone balustrades punctuated by geranium-filled urns, shingle paths wandered through the fragrant shrubbery, and at the heart of it all was a fountain without which no Italian garden is complete.

The only disappointment was the swimming pool. It was the most decrepit area of the whole place, broken tiles peeling paintwork and rusty iron steps and handrails all combined to discourage any inclination to take a dip. We returned to the shady terrace and the luxury of a quiet read. The interlude did not last long but was brought to an abrupt end by the onset of a storm, an explanation for the morning's lassitude. There was hardly any warning, just a sudden darkening of the sky, ricocheting lightning cracking across the valley and then the rain came in one saturating deluge. There was hardly time to run for cover.

How changed the villa was now in the premature dusk. The mellow antiquity was no longer attractive, but gloomy, even menacing and the deserted corridors and public rooms appeared forbiddingly sombre without the gilding sunlight. In all this silence, it came as something of a shock when a gong resounded through the entire house, the summons to dine. Ah! we thought, dinner will lighten the atmosphere but there we were wrong, it was actually worse.

The meal was served in an austere refectory-like room reminiscent of a monastery, and the small gathering of guests (the first we had seen) by their silence, could have been a community of monks tied by strict vows. The stillness was almost tangible. The melancholy atmosphere called to mind a vivid literary image. In the Castle of Crossed Destinies, Italo Calvine brings together a group of travellers who seek shelter at an inn on just such a night as this. By some strange fluke, they all find themselves bereft of speech, but the urge to exchange stories is strong and one of the party finds a solution with the aid of a pack of tarot cards. He proceeds to tell of his adventures through the medium of the cards followed in turn by each of his companions. But we had no tarot cards!

To add to the discomfort the food was indifferent, which is a polite way of saying that it was poor, and it was served by a dour unsmiling creature that surely would have punished anyone guilty of leaving food uneaten, or of speaking above a whisper. Even the wine failed to loosen the tongues.

The rest of that weird stormy evening was spent on further forays into the 'hinterland' of this strange villa. We unearthed another public room on the upper floor that might once have been the games and leisure centre of house parties in the glorious past. It was unoccupied, ill lit and anything but festive with an overwhelming smell of dust and decay. Stiff unwelcoming chairs lined the walls that were hung with the usual mottled mirrors and the usual dark ancestral portraits. The piano was very locked, and the billiard table shrouded with neither balls nor cues thus ensuring that no music or games would disturb the ghosts in the shadows of this forgotten place.

Our own room was hardly less sinister with shutters closed against the storm and a flickering light from inadequate lamps. At least we were lucky not to be subjected to a power cut. That would have been the last straw. There was nothing for it but to resort to sleep, and we were relieved to discover that the matromoniale was both clean and comfortable and despite the thunder, howling wind and rattling shutters we were soon insensible, undisturbed by any hint of nightmare.

In the morning, we lacked the stamina to face further intimidation in the bleak refectory and set off breakfastless. The storm had passed leaving a very wet world that glittered in pale watery sunlight and a road awash with steaming puddles. One thing was certain, Villa Casanova was the most original hostelry we ever experienced and would not be forgotten and as we turned at the head of the valley for a final view of its ochre walls, red pantiled roof and dark green shutters, we reflected upon its future. How long could this relic of a bygone era, this curiosity, survive the pressures of the video and computer age?

This was now the proverbial last ditch, we were desperate to stop the wandering existence and came to the conclusion that we must follow the advice offered by the estate agent to look for a place at the resorts, starting with Viareggio. We had to retrace the first part of the route past Lucca and endured a pang or two of regret for that particular abandoned dream. The morning's weak sunlight soon gave way to another crop of thunderous looking clouds, and then the rain came, such rain as we would prefer not to encounter very often. At Viareggio, we had no choice but to pull off the flooded road that was axle deep in places and wait hopefully for an improvement. Fortunately, though sharp the downpour was short and we were able to carry on.

Viareggio looked forlorn as only a holiday resort at the end of the season, and in the rain, can look. Nothing would induce us to make this a permanent base, not while we still had the strength to persevere in the search for a real home in a living town. The idea of renting an apartment in an empty tower block was horrifying; we would give up and go home first even if it meant the admission of defeat. The coast westward continued in much the same vein, being a succession of Lidos and Marinas with miles of marshalled beach chairs looking utterly forlorn in the wet. It was excruciatingly boring. That is, until the road began to climb over the Passo di Bracco, the Cinqueterre promontory. It is a beautiful region of forested hills and extensive views and the boisterous weather conditions made a lively panorama. Racing cloud shadows alternated with bright patches of sunlight and the stiff breeze transformed the forested slopes into rolling breakers, like a wind whipped ocean. The change of scene and weather suited us; it was just what we needed to spur us on to final effort.

The western side of the promontory contrasted completely with the previous stretch of coast. Here the towns were graceful, with elegant buildings and promenades lined with palm trees, tamarisk, oleander and other exotics. It was a constantly repeated tableau of beauty. Why we failed to stop and try our luck at Sestri Levante or Rapallo or any of the others seems completely irrational when viewed in retrospect but for some reason we made a choice from the map and the guide-book and inflexibly stuck to it. This magnet that lured us on so relentlessly was Spotorno, described in our trusted source of information as a charming small fishing port just beyond the town of Savona, and to this vision we clung regardless of the glories through which we passed.

Genoa was something of a nightmare to negotiate. This important port of three-quarters of a million inhabitants is compressed laterally along a ten-mile long narrow shelf between high mountains and the sea. Being a port means that it is the focal point of heavy goods lorries from all over Italy and beyond and it was our job to negotiate a way through this compressed traffic. It was good to clear the commercial sprawl and for some distance all was serene as we passed through Varezzi, Celle, Albisola Marina, (this last being the home of Majolica pottery), and then into Savona.

Another rainstorm in conjunction with rush hour traffic caused a few nasty moments, but we emerged without incident. Spotorno was now close and my pulse rate rose with apprehension. I could not believe that a satisfactory end was really within our grasp, sensing only another disillusion. And it was so. We has used the C.I.T. brochure's information in this instance and could only assume that they were a little out of date, because the little fishing port was no more, having been submerged by massive modern development and all the paraphernalia that goes to the making of a modern tourist resort. We felt cheated as though the fault lay with someone else, not ourselves.

Thoroughly weary we drove on in a semi-stupor, more by instinct than design having fallen victim to the old bugbear of vacuity in perpetual motion. We mentally kicked ourselves at the thought of places passed and disregarded, but it was too late to do anything about them now. Old habits die hard they say and so it was with us, for even at this apparent impasse we automatically studied the map and indifferently made one final attempt to track down this figment of our imagination. Three miles and one rocky headland lay between us and Noli, and like the fisherman and his proverbial last cast, we flung all our hopes into those three miles. Miraculously it paid off and we hooked a great prize for round the final bend, we discovered Noli, Antica Republica Marinara. It was like a microcosm of all Italy, an exquisite town nestling in a minute crescent-shaped bay, the incarnation of a romantic mental image.

81

Chapter Six

Via Fiumara

'The river is within us, the sea is all about us'.   *T S Eliot.*

The speed with which we became householders was unbelievable, when you consider what this entailed. Finding an agent, making a short list of property available and then the final selection was all accomplished by lunch on the first morning. After the trauma of deciding upon an area and narrowing this down to an actual place, the choosing of accommodation was like child's play. The Agencia di Affiti was run by an obliging man and wife team called Valentino who took us round to view various rooms and then produced requisite agreement forms for us to sign and the keys were ours. The rent of 136,000 lira per month was almost laughably small being the equivalent of about £16 per week. We couldn't believe our good fortune and walked around with heads in the clouds for the rest of the day.

There was a slight delay over moving into the apartment on Via Fiumara while the owner gave the rooms a thorough going over even though they looked immaculate. But this was normal practice as we were to find whenever we leased a place from a bedsit to a villa in Spain. We had three rooms, a large bedroom a dining kitchen and bathroom, all well appointed and equipped, and at last we could unpack all the personal belongings that had travelled with us for six weeks hidden in the depths of Fulvia's luggage boot.

The early days were spent settling into a workable routine and finding our bearings. Being scarcely a mile long and only slightly more in depth, the history of this tiny republic is all the more remarkable. Maritime civilisation is recorded in the region as a whole as far back as 200 BC, the numerous deep-water bays being perfectly workable as natural harbours, and it is fairly certain that Noli figured prominently in those early sea-faring activities. In the Middle Ages, it was of Byzantine allegiance in opposition to the Longobards, then a stronghold against the Saracens and later it is recorded as playing an important role in the first Crusade as a port of embarkation. Dante lived here for a time and is reputed to have dashed off a few cantos of La Comedia; (my guess is that this was his inspiration for the final Paradise verses). Columbus sailed from the port of Noli with a fleet of five ships on one of his many expeditions, and Galileo too comes indirectly in for a mention through his ill-fated disciple Giordano Bruno, a man who taught here and was subsequently burnt at the stake for his enlightened views.

The most outstanding date, and that closest to the hearts of present day Nolians is August 7th 1193, the birth of the Republic. A revolution led by the Marquis Henry del Carrette resulted from a meeting held in the shadow of the ancient Romanesque church of San Paragorio. The church still stands in a quiet corner of the town and is a popular venue for fashionable weddings.

The historic gathering of rebellious citizens decreed that Genoa should no longer rule over them, and the tiny republic that emerged prospered against all the odds for over six centuries. It was a Diocesan centre from 1239 to 1820 and was ruled by model commune constitutions, an achievement that is commemorated annually with the celebration of the Regate des Quartiers. Teams of oarsmen from each of the four quarters of the town, Portellu, Maina, Ciassa, and Burgu, challenge each other in a grand regatta before an audience of town dignitaries. All parties are each splendidly turned out in medieval costume and to add to the fun there are processions, bands, special music in the churches and a great deal of outdoor feasting.

The Maritime Republic flourished up to Napoleon's time when the Ligurian Democratic Republic was founded, and in 1815 resulting from the Congress of Vienna, they were annexed along with Piemonte to the Kingdom of Sardinia. A marked individualism is still palpable within the tightly knit community but it has become necessary to bend with the wind of change and centralism and they are now part of the province of Savona.

The heyday of the small port is long since over, 20th century commerce demanding the complex facilities of the great ports such as Genoa. All that remains of the maritime tradition is a handful of small fishing boats, each with a crew of four, five, or six men who eke out a precarious living still following the traditional methods of their ancestors. A whole night's work could sometimes bring in nothing but a handful or two of sardines, but there were good times when the tunny were running and somehow or other, with the aid of co-operatives, the good times subsidised the bad. Many of the men had seasonal hotel jobs by day and fished by night so when they ever managed to snatch some sleep was a complete mystery.

Noli's physical situation at the western end of the deeply curving Italian Riviera, the Riviera di Ponente, has certain disadvantages as a winter residence because of its easterly aspect. But this fact was not yet obvious to us as new residents. The sun still shone every day and would seem to go on forever with every rock and wall and terraced hillside vibrating and reflecting the lovely reliable warmth. Exploratory walks were a joy amongst a wealth of autumn wild flowers. The colours were predominately blue and mauve with wild leeks, giant bellflowers and an abundance of chicory and once we came upon an entire meadow of autumn crocus and saffron. Wonderful aromatic scents were released as we unavoidably trampled thyme and basil and mint underfoot. There were many unusual insects too. Brilliant blue and red grasshoppers, humming-bird moths, blue bees and that incredible creature the praying mantis. Shrewd eyed lizards rustled amongst the drystone walls of terraces where vines were heavy with fruit and the leaves made a vivid splash of red or gold, and occasionally we disturbed small brown snakes sunning themselves in the dust. Who could give a thought to the winter solstice sun in this little Eden? We were too busy enjoying the present to imagine a time when this idyllic valley would be out of reach of the sun's warmth and even with that knowledge I doubt if there would have been a moment's regret for the choice we made. To us Noli was, and still in memory remains, perfection, a red-roofed gem set in a green cleft at the edge of a diminutive bay of cobalt blue water. We were hemmed in by gentle slopes of olive and cypress and vine.

We had a castle, a bishop's palace, a cathedral, a curtain-wall, ramparts and towers all in a neatly circumscribed space that was within easy walking distance. At the northern end Noli is protected from winter winds by Monte Ursino, a hill upon which the ruined castle of the commune period stands, and from here the curtain wall descends the steep slope to join the town's encircling ramparts. About halfway down this south-facing hillside is the old palace of the former bishops, now used as a youth hostel, and the open space in front of this building was an admirable vantage point and sun-trap. From here you could look out over the roof tops of the whole town, count all five of the towers of nobility dating back to the 13th century, and check the not quite synchronised time on the clock towers of cathedral and townhall as they chimed their respective quarters. According to ancient records, 72 towers once stood in Noli but I cannot imagine how they would all fit in.

The short section of the Via Aurelia that crosses the seafront is a fine avenue of oleander, tamarisk and fat little palm trees, and the parallel promenade is brilliant with flower beds and outdoor cafés. The equivalent notice of our English 'Please do not walk on the grass' was here 'Non calpestare le aiuole' which roughly translated is 'do not stamp on the flowerbeds'. The buildings along the Via Aurelia are a handsome mix of ancient and modern, a successful blend that unites old and new architecture. Through a central arched gateway, you enter the old town, a warren of narrow cobbled streets leading in and out of irregular shaped piazzas.

Everywhere the streets are lined with small cave like shops that overflow with goods and produce; fruit and vegetables, bread and pastas, wine, cheese, meat, and the most delicious cakes and pastries. The aroma along these lanes was almost a feast in itself, a tantalising olfactory feast.

One evening during our first week in Noli, we met a young American couple and enjoyed our first English conversation for many weeks. It was the hour before restaurants open and aperitifs were filling the void, a situation conducive to easy conversation, an interchange of our respective projects. Our own enterprise was relegated to the shade when we learned that this enthusiastic pair were launched on the Grand Tour – from Britain to Greece on bicycles. A few days later we had another encounter in English, this time with contemporary Australians who were also touring Europe but by coach. Newly arrived in Italy they were experiencing difficulty over filling out a cheque in the bank, the formidable superfluity of zeros being the stumbling block that takes time to overcome and accept as a matter of course. Our paths crossed again a day or two later in the thick of the market-day crowd we greeted each other like old friends and lost no time in arranging a meeting that night at one of the passeggio cafés. It was a marvellous pleasure to swap traveller's tales with ones equals in both age and language and as it turned out it was the last opportunity for such indulgence. The Australians left Noli the next day for another leg of their tour, and as the season was virtually over, we settled down to the real period of integration.

During the conversation with Keith and Beth, our Aussie friends, they described an interesting visit they had made to caves know as the Grottos de Toirano, in the hills a short distance from Loano. On their recommendation we made the trip ourselves and were not disappointed. The mountains in this region being limestone are honeycombed with subterranean passages and caves, and two extensive sections of these had recently been opened to the public. Almost a mile in extent the Basura and St. Lucia caves are extremely good examples of water erosion sculpture. The amazingly grotesque and often very beautiful passages and cathedral-like chambers are crammed with stalagmites and stalactites. The variety of shape and form is quite astonishing from tall and slender to squat and bulbous, pencil slim fragility and robust elephantinism, and some really exquisite filigree-fine tower-like constructions. One cave was known as the organ gallery and here the guide tapped out a tune on a row of 'pipes' that gave a convincing musical sound. In another gallery, the centuries of dripping water had sculpted a weird exhibition to satisfy the keenest advocate of the avant-garde. An ingenious lighting system heightened the effect on the dripping vari-coloured rock formations, producing a glittering ethereal fantasyland. There were indications that some of the caves had been used as habitations in prehistoric times. We were shown fossilised bones of early cavebears and the petrified footprint of a man said to be of the Neanderthal period as well as certain signs of firebrands that were thought to be those of torches.

October came and with it the local vendemmia. Noli was rich with the scents of fermentation making every breath intoxication, a brush with Bacchus. The weather continued fine, mellow days following one another with euphoric repetition, mellow days in which we swam and walked and explored Liguria to the east, the west, and the mountainous hinterland. Then without warning the rains came, not just an hour or two, or even a day but a continuing deluge that on the third morning had us worried. On this particular morning, we woke to an unfamiliar sound, a gushing, poppling swashing sound of running water that had us out of bed in a panic. When we flung open the shutters and looked down onto the Via Fiumara the road had disappeared to be replaced by a river of racing mud-brown water. Fiumara means river and now we understood its origin, we were living on a torrente, the course of a mountain flash-flood that was channelled between the ramparts of the old town and some more recent developments, of which our block was one, built on a slight rise at the foot of the south cliff.

The rain continued and we watched fascinated as the river continued to rise bringing with it all the flotsam and jetsam of floodwaters. We wondered how on earth we were to get over the river for supplies. There was nothing in the kitchen as we were in the habit of living on a day to day basis, being so close to the shops but now it looked as though we were in for a hungry day, or even longer judging by the unremitting downpour. Then through the veils of rain, an apparition appeared enveloped from head to foot in shiny yellow oilskins and sea boots. He was joined by another similarly clad figure and then a third and between them, they trundled an unwieldy wooden contraption perched on top of huge iron-rimmed wheels. Slowly it was manoeuvred into position across the fast flowing river and low and behold, we had an improvised footbridge. This then was not a unique happening; the authorities were ready with their lifeline, a wonderful if somewhat primitive contrivance for the relief of the fringe dwellers. Needless to say, we took instant advantage of the novel footbridge to lay in food and drink to withstand a siege.

By evening the rain had stopped, and the following morning our river had dwindled to an insignificant trickle. The swift end to the drama was quite an anticlimax. Once we were released from the temporary incarceration we had begun to enjoy the excitement of watching the racing water from our safe vantage point. But the change in the weather was welcome nevertheless. The return of blue sky and glittering sunlight inspired plans for a long deferred expedition to visit Venice.

Options vary amongst Italophiles as to which city has the greatest claim to supremacy. Each has its loyal devotees who squander praise upon one while denigrating another. In a letter to his sister Fanny, Mendelssohn wrote that Venice was a mouldering pile, the mosaics nothing but Turkish tinsel on top of mildewed cement. But Rome, ah Rome! However one man's jaundiced vision, even though the man be Mendelssohn could not put us off our ambition to visit the city of a hundred and seventeen islands, mildew or no mildew. We already had Rome, Florence, Pisa, Bologna and

Milan under our belts and were looking forward to notching up the unique city of Venice.

Exhilarated by the prospect of taking to the road again especially with such a destination, we packed a few indispensables, filled the cool box with the recently appropriated siege supplies, and away we went. The total distance, taking the mountain road from Savona to Alessandria, then east across the Po plain was roughly 300 miles which given reasonable traffic and road conditions we reckoned on covering in one day. All went well until the last ten miles, the approach to Chioggia where we planned to spend the night. The weather that had inspired us by its perfection at the onset now turned extremely nasty. A violent squall blew in from the Adriatic bringing torrents of rain and hurricane force winds against which we made little more than walking speed. Add to that homebound traffic and early darkness, and we began to have doubts about the sense of our purpose, but Chioggia loomed out of the darkness and we set about the search for somewhere to spend the night.

We were soon soaked to the skin as we battled against the tearing wind, hampered in our quest by the lack of light and a feeling of disorientation resulting from violent and almost continuous thunder. This must have been the fourth or fifth such storm we had experienced in the two and a half months since coming south. Not what we had expected at all. Albergo Clodia, when we found it, was a true haven from the storm, and to our relief it boasted a small restaurant so we need not leave our shelter again that night. Life didn't look half so bad when we had dried out and were sitting in front of a piping hot bowl of good minestrone well laced with parmesan cheese. There was no fault to be found with the veal steaks and fresh salad nor the superb bowl of fruit, so once again food and warmth restored the body and with it came reassurance of the wisdom of the enterprise, come what may.

There was no need to hurry over the meal; on the contrary, we spun it out at a leisurely pace eavesdropping on a nearby conversation, that of a trio of men, who by their rugged appearance could well have been fishermen. As they consumed enormous plates-full of shellfish, they argued about the current political crisis. We grasped that the government was on the point of collapse, a not infrequent situation at the time, and a question was raised that struck me as philosophically profound. It was an idea that appealed to our apolitical esprit and went along the lines of; 'So the government goes again, does life stop? Do we not go on working and playing, eating and sleeping, so should we worry ourselves into an early grave? No, amico mio, Italy will still be here with or without government'.

We went to bed early. There was nothing else to do and in any case, it was our intention to make a prompt start in the morning, but sleep at first was difficult because of the noise from the continuing storm. Lightning flashed spasmodically, penetrating the ill-fitting shutters while the wind tore at them with such demonic fury that we wondered how long they could take the strain and remain intact. But eventually we slept and somehow or other the shutters survived and were still in place when we woke. The storm had passed leaving a calm bright dawn.

We breakfasted quickly, being impatient to see something of our whereabouts but we could not spare too much of this special day, therefore the reconnaissance was restricted to the hotel's immediate locality, which turned out to be close to the banks of the main canal. Chioggia has the reputation of being the poor man's Venice, being likewise water-based with its network of canals. But Palazzi are few and commerce constitutes the greater part of the water-borne traffic.

The canal was incredibly busy and as we approached from the street at right angles to it, all we could see was a great confusion of moving masts and rigging. Those closest to us on the right-hand bank were making their stately way in from the sea, and the contra-flow on the left bank was the day fleet on the way out. We followed the course of the incoming fleet and thus discovered the largest and most diverse fish market we had seen. It was exciting to be a spectator amongst such intense activity as was enacted here, the constant movement, the quantity, the variety and colour. Nothing seemed to be too large or too small to be worthy of culinary use, yet I found myself wondering if this vast quantity of seafood would find its way onto someone's plate. It was mind-bending.

By eight thirty, we were crossing the flat land alongside the Venetian lagoons, and there she was, caught between sea and sky, the distant city rising mirage-like from calm waters. Beyond the city and even more ethereal, a range of snow-capped mountains made a perfect backdrop against the newly washed sky. We could not have wished for a greater effect for our approach.

We crossed the three-mile long road bridge that funnels all vehicles into an enormous peripheral car park and waited, not very patiently, for a space. It was not as bad as it looked for in less than half an hour we were aboard the vaporetto on the way to St. Mark's square. I can still recall the sense of awe, the choking emotion that overcame me as each well-known painting and photograph came to life around us. It was an unfamiliar sensation, I was not normally given to such extreme sensitivity, appreciative yes but this was quite out of character. It may have been something to do with the atmosphere, the luminous quality of the October light after rain, or the startling affect of diverging sunlight that bounced off water and marble and gilded mosaic. The reality outshone even the greatest artistic representation.

I make no attempt to give a guide book description of what we observed of Venice, there are better ones available than I could possibly hope to achieve, so what follows are a few impressions from that first intoxicating vaporetto ride to sunset over San Giorgio. The transitory scenes of the busy canals, the dynamic impact of the Doges' Palace, St. Mark's Basilica and the elegant piazza, coffee at Florians, an irresistible extravagance for the sake of its famous association; Byron, Goethe, George Sand, Wagner and others, everything lived up to expectations. We bought sandwiches and spring water for an al fresco lunch, utilising stacked boardwalks with which footpaths are raised when the water floods over canal banks. They made quite serviceable seating and were in constant demand by the multi-national crowd. The frugal lunch was followed by sumptuous window shopping in the marzaria quarter. It is an Aladdin's cave of tiny but fabulous shops displaying luxury goods of lace, jewellery, glass, and the distinctive ebony statuary and black and gold furniture that belongs exclusively to Venice. What would I not have given for an open cheque? There followed a wonderful quiet hour along silent out of the way places, the silent labyrinth of rose-brick squares and hump-backed bridges. We penetrated flagstone streets losing ourselves amongst the lesser flower-decked palaces but by mid-afternoon the feet began to protest and we were forced to call a halt and find somewhere to recuperate.

It was fortunate that the church of Santa Maria dei Frari was close by, not a bad place to relax. On consulting the Green Guide we learned that this was the largest church in Venice and that it contained some notable works of art which included two magnificent Titian altarpieces, the north aisle contained the Virgin of the Pesaro family, and above the high alter is the magnificent Assumption. If our aching feet had not demanded respite, how easily we could have missed this opportunity. Quite close to Santa Maria we noticed the three star Scuola di San Rocco, a 16C Renaissance building said to contain an outstanding collection of Tintoretto's, but it was no use attempting a gallery visit under the circumstances so we had to be content with the façade and its fluted columns and arches and friezes, not such a poor compromise to have to settle for.

It was time to refuel again with fruit from a stall and panforte from an elegant cake shop, the elegance reflected in the price of 2,000 lire, almost twice what we had paid in Sienna. The cake made us thirsty so next priority was a tea shop, another excuse to take the weight off our feet and then it was almost dusk and time to board the last 'bus' home along the Canal Grande. Another never to be forgotten elevated moment came with the crossing of the Bacino di San Marco at sunset with its convoys of gliding gondolas and brisk motoscafi silhouetted against the pellucid light. We reclaimed the car from Piazzale Roma and slowly drove away with the words Horas non-numero nisi serenas (I count only the happy hours) an inscription on a sundial, ringing in our ears. It was the most perfectly apt sentiment for our day.

It was hard to tear ourselves away but we had been unable to find suitable accommodation in the city, a city whose season does not end. Consequently we recrossed the causeway and took the road to Treviso. We had not far to go before finding a reasonable wayside motel but it was non-catering, which meant further trekking in search of food. The receptionist's recommendation was 'Just a short way along the road' but we hobbled for twenty agonising minutes before the goal was reached. And then we were almost too tired to eat. I have no recollection of what we ate or how we got back to the hotel, but I do remember the next morning.

We could hardly believe our eyes or our incredible luck for we opened the shutters to overcast skies and steady rain. The perfect gem of a day had emerged sandwiched between the grey gloom of this and the preceding storm in Chioggia. What could we do but thank the charitable Gods for giving us that one glorious day. It could so easily have been ruined. As it was the journey home by way of two more noble cites, Vicenza and Verona was disappointing as the rain spoilt our hopes of sightseeing. It was a case of crawling as slowly as traffic would allow through the cities to peer myopically through misted windows and pouring rain, not the most sat-isfactory arrangement. We reached Noli with the last daylight, tired but content. It had been an altogether successful expe-dition that had increased our love for and awareness of this great country.

The rains of October continued on and off bringing snow to the higher reaches of the Ligurian Apennines but with November there returned a settled period of calm warm days when sea swimming was possible albeit rather more invigorating than relaxing. Nights too were much colder. On one particular sharp evening, Signor Valentino appeared armed with a pile of extra blankets, bedside rugs, and an electric convector heater for which we were extremely thankful. The general run of the Mediterranean habitation is designed to keep cool in summer with no concessions to the winter months. It is the shortest season; therefore, not worthy of consideration would seem to be the general consensus.

With the onset of winter, new diversions opened up with the advent of concerts in both Savona the regional capital, and the neighbouring town of Finale Ligure. The first of these was given by a Ukrainian dance company who were there at the special invitation of the civic authorities in Savona. To our surprise, there was no charge for admission. It was financed as a mark of goodwill by the municipality in the beautiful neo-classical Teatro Chiabrera. And a splendidly exuberant performance it was. At the conclusion, there were long rambling speeches of mutual admiration given by both town dignitaries and concert officials in both Italian and Russian. To say we were confused is putting it mildly; the double translation required was an intellectual exercise beyond our limited grasp of Italian, and the little we made of it failed to explain the humour that rocked the audience. Still the bonhomie rubbed off and we enjoyed being a part of it.

The next event was a symphony concert by an orchestra from Genoa with Ruggiero Ricci playing the solo violin in a celebratory programme entirely devoted to the works of Paganini. This was one of a series to mark the bicentenary of the composer's birth in Genoa and proved to be a stimulating and very enjoyable performance. Finale Ligure was the venue of a monthly piano recital. It was a series given in a charming small concert room by young international competition winners and we listened to some wonderfully promising recitals by these young musicians, many of whom would be destined for great honours in their own countries if not on the concert platforms of the world. All these evenings played an important part in the process of our integration as the bond between ourselves and fellow concertgoers was strengthened through the common language of music. It was the beginning of real involvement when the imputation 'tourist' could justifiably be shaken off. I never minded the epithet traveller but that could only be claimed when on the move and now our desire was to be considered residents.

Our only regret was the lack of opportunity to make real contact with like-minded people, the difficulties that stood in the way of friendship. At this stage, encounters were pleasant but superficial and occasionally we wished for something more. Our main source of contact was a somewhat stilted gossip up on the piazzale of the old palace of the bishops where many of the older residents spent their afternoons basking in what was probably the warmest spot in Noli including their own apartments. It was a good place to work at some tapestry or read or write letters. It was a useful place at which to draw breath in the steep climb to the hilltop cemetery being about the half way stage, consequently there was invariably a clutch of black-clad widows on their way to deposit floral tributes at the graves of their loved ones. But there was no gloom. Death was only acknowledged by their garb but not by their demeanour.

One day we fell into conversation with an American lady who must have been in her early fifties, and she told us something of her life and problems. Like us, she was an ardent Italophile but unlike us had no partner with whom to share that passion, being either widowed or divorced, I can't remember which but the fact remains that she was alone. She had been working as a librarian at the International School in Milan, had been made redundant, and was now desperately looking for work in one of the catering language schools that trained staff for the hotels in the tourist regions. Unfortunately English was not in demand this being a predominately German holiday venue and meanwhile she was without income, living in a cramped caravan and eating sparingly of only the cheapest of seasonal food from the market. She could have admitted defeat and returned to live with a sister in America but this was the life she loved and refused to relinquish without a struggle. I have often wondered what became of that plucky American lady hoping that a job turned up in time to save her way of life, but our paths did not cross again.

The reason for this is that not long after hearing her story we had our own problems. It was December and a letter from home brought an end to this phase of our experiment in opting out. Someone else's need meant an imminent return to family responsibility that could not be ignored. For five months we had lived only for ourselves, had learnt a lot, sometimes the hard way, but there was no doubt in our minds that this hitch would only be temporary and as soon as the uncomfortable situation back home had been rectified we would be back on the trail. The Lancia resumed her former role of home base, packed once more to the gunwhales and we set out on a wintry crossing of France to reach home on the run down to Christmas.

Vestnes Prestegard, the first of many havens

The author with Dino and Olga at Castel d'Aiano

Villa Casenova (Lucca) before the storm

Venice, after the storm

Taormina, the Three Legs of Man mystery

Andalusia's National Day, as celebrated in Almunecar

Casa Anonyma, the last but not least of our havens

Lancia Fulvia en route to Sicily

Chapter Seven

Back on the Road

'Travelling is the ruin of all happiness. There's no looking at a building after seeing Italy'.

Fanny Burney.

Eight months passed, during which we celebrated the birth of a first grandchild, mourned the death of a stepfather, and rejoiced at the marriage of a second son. Meanwhile, the economic tangle of another son, the cause of our hasty return to the UK the previous winter had been satisfactorily resolved. At the end of August we were at last free to pick up the threads and resume the experiment.

Arrangements were promptly finalised to make the crossing from Newhaven to Dieppe on the 28th of the month, the day after the aforementioned wedding. France sparkled and shimmered in the late summer heat, a marked contrast to her grim winter profile remembered from our last encounter when snow and ice had been the order of the day. Conditions were perfect for meandering across country by minor roads rather than making a headlong rush by the direct route.

The first night stop was Chartres, the Hotel Metropole on Rue de Bourg Neuf, a useful staging post strategically placed for access to and from ports with the added advantage of being very cheap. It was also within easy reach of the attractive old town and the magnificent cathedral, the massive Notre-Dame that Rodin is reputed to have dubbed 'L'acropole de la France'. The timing of our approach to the cathedral could not have been bettered. It was sunset and the façade was bathed in a stunning unnatural brilliance with flying buttresses gargoyles, arches, towers and stylised stone saints all turned to gold. Midas himself could not have used his magic touch to better effect. But all reverted to stone with the going down of the sun, as though at the flick of a switch.

From Chartres we followed a lovely stretch of the Loire, castle spotting. Chenonceaux, Valencay, Langeais and Amboise slipped in and out of the route with pleasurable ease, all so elegant and somehow feminine in their fairytale settings. The pale gold and dusty green landscape resulting from the hot dry summer complimented the silver-grey of the chateaux perfectly and the parks and gardens were a great temptation to dawdle.

Then followed the long haul up into the rugged Massif Centrale, the remote heartland of France. Night caught us out miles from any possibility of finding an auberge but the weather was mild and the situation a camper's dream. Besides which we were fresh from civilisation and welcomed the idea of spending a night so close to the wilderness and so far from the madding crowd. There was plenty of food aboard and a stream close at hand for rustic ablutions, we felt confidently foolproof.

But the morning after we came as close to disaster as I ever wish to be on a journey. We had forgotten the restrictions of reclined car seats when space has to be shared with half a ton of luggage. We had forgotten how you long to change position, turn over, anything to give relief to tired limbs, to relieve the cramping pressure. We were consequently up with the lark but not as chirpy. Eric felt decidedly under the weather but said nothing as he took himself off for a recuperative walk while I tidied the car and prepared breakfast.

The situation that followed could be described as the traveller's nightmare, being stricken by illness in the middle of nowhere. Defensively we quote, 'it is not likely to happen to us' but of course it can, and sometimes does. Out of sight of the car, Eric collapsed. He said afterwards that without warning he went out like a light and consequently was unable to take evasive action as it were, but fell flat on his face. His long absence made me uneasy and following the direction he had taken, I found him just as he was coming round. He looked terrible, as though he'd just done ten rounds in the ring with a blockbusting heavyweight who had concentrated the onslaught on his face. There was blood on his forehead, nose and mouth. For an instant I froze, fear paralysing everything except my thumping heart that went berserk. I began to pick up the bits; a denture minus a tooth, spectacles with a cracked bridge but lenses intact, and gradually I stopped shaking, pulled myself together and ran back for the car. By the time, I got back to the scene the patient was sitting up and able to heave himself with a little help into the passenger seat. My first fear of a heart attack remained, and the thought of doctors, or worse still, hospital whirled round in my mind as I mentally dredged up my inadequate school French. The crisis passed the attack proving to be nothing worse than a severe dose of cramp exacerbated by dehydration. A wash in the mountain stream and a massive intake of spring-water plus copious supplies of tea and Eric was as good as new. He took a rest from the rigours of driving to complete the cure. It was a sobering experience for both of us.

This all happened somewhere in the region of the Ardeche, between le Puy and Privas and from there we crossed the Rhone valley and were well on the way to the High Alps. The day passed quietly as I drove at a very easy pace through Crest, Die, and Gap and towards evening at the village of le Lauzet Ubaye on the edge of an emerald green lake, we decided to make this our bolthole for the night. Provided of course that the village could rise to an auberge because on no account could we consider another night sleeping 'wild'. The situation was irresistible, the green lake fringed with rushes and willows that gave onto softer green pastures in which cattle grazed, then pine forested hillsides and rising high above these the soul-stirring towering peaks. It would have been difficult to select a more appropriate spot in which to complete the convalescence had we a dozen to choose from and this was purely fortuitous.

The only inn was at the far end of the village facing the lake, and although a little dingy and down at heel, the beds were fine and the food surprisingly good. Trout fresh from the green lake embellished with garlic and mushrooms more than compensated for the 'traditional' antiquated plumbing. A tranquil stroll by the water's edge in the twilight with distant peaks catching the last rosy glow of sunset was a reassuring end to a day that had dawned so dramatically.

The fine weather continued, the morning being ideal for the assault on Col de Larche leading into Italy and the decent of the Maddalena. Eric was now back at the helm for this the ultimate day of the return journey, the Ligurian coast was now well within our sights.

The alpine scenery of that long climb and descent had us on the edge of our seats in more ways than one. It had everything: magnificence, desolation, grandeur, savagery AND a terrible road surface. Sensational vistas flashed by as we jolted and bumped over the ice-damaged tarmac down the perpetual steps of nerve-wracking hairpin bends. We passed a lonely frontier post, a dark place of gloomy crags and harsh scree-slopes surrounding a shantytown, the last outpost of civilisation. Bored officials and shadowy bystanders seemed unreal as though not wholly of this world. A little further on the road overlooked a valley that was almost entirely sub-merged in skeletal apartment blocks, dumps of cement, gird-ers, bricks, giant cranes, cement mixers, in fact a building site of mammoth proportions. It turned out to be an embry-onic ski station, another money-spinner for the developers that was not only spoiling a great environment but upsetting the equilibrium. Our age of leisure has a lot to answer for.

In stark contrast to the raw newness of the ski village was the first old Italian village. It was situated in a narrow gorge; a windswept godforsaken place hemmed in by high rock walls that inhibited light and warmth from the sun. Houses of crumbling stucco and peeling paint told of poverty and hopelessness, and the few inhabitants seemed almost hostile as they followed with cold eyes our progress through their mountain fastness. We might have been aliens from outer space according to their expression of recoil. Not for the first time, we wondered how such a community made its living and why such an inhospitable site was ever colonised in the beginning.

A few hours later we entered Finale Ligure, a lively Riviera resort about ten kilometres west of Noli, which after due consideration regarding aspect and amenities was now our preferred venue for the initial base-camp. The 1982 tour as an experiment had taught us to moderate the wanderlust and establish a 'home' before setting out on exploratory journeys. And to be frank, there had been some pressure from family who had not really approved of the weeks we had wandered O.N.F.A. Despite the fact that the season was still in full swing, we found a room at the tucked away Albergo Italia from which to start house hunting.

One of Finale's great attractions was its 'real town' atmosphere. It enjoys a fine south facing aspect at the foot of the western chain of the Apennines. It is a colourful town of three distinct sections that span two river valleys. Marina is the central section and this straddles the Via Aurelia which separates the esplanade and old town from later development that tends to climb in steep terraces up the face of the cliff between the two valleys. The eastern sector, Finale Pia, has a more open aspect at the head of a wide river gorge that opens out into a spacious tree-lined piazza. To complete the trio, Finale Borgo, one and a half miles up the western river, and the most interesting historically of the three. It was a former capital of the marquisate and still maintains a certain air of panache with its turrets and grand Gothic Collegiate church built into a tower in the walls. The elegant campanile is particularly worthy of note. Altogether the town promised plenty of interest and we set about the search for accommodation with enthusiasm.

Three days of viewing was interesting in itself with a tremendously mixed bag of properties. They ranged from basic holiday flats, sixth floor and no lift, to crumbling antiquity reeking of neglect, but fortunately we were not reduced to either extremity being presented with an adequate compromise. In Finale Pia we found a good first floor apartment in a modern residential block at the moderate price of £125 per month, and this also gave us parking space and quiet surroundings.

Our new address was Via Castelli, a road that circles the cliff that splits the two valleys, at the summit of which stands the inevitable ruined castle. We were conveniently placed for shops or seashore or upland walks and in no time at all we had settled in and embarked on the enthralling process of familiarisation. Every day brought fresh discoveries, and new revelations intermingled with such favourite activities as a daily swim and that wonderful Mediterranean pastime, 'ambulante' on the esplanade watching the world go by. But we also liked to escape from the town and the busy coast road to the peaceful hinterland.

On one of these away from it all walks, we traced the track of the old Roman road of the Ponti Romani. Although this may once have been a busy thoroughfare, it has become little more than an overgrown track that pushes its way through rugged hill-country. The name Via Emilia conjures up the one time glory of an empire as though sometime in its history, the road enjoyed a certain prestige, but now wild nature is its only glory. Following the track up through orchards of peach trees, olives, and higher still, dense forests of chestnut, we came to the first of the five Roman bridges. This one was in an excellent state of preservation and still carried the old road across a stream. It had all the hallmarks of Rome, slim red brick topped off by neatly dressed stone blocks that are held firmly in place by that remarkable substance, Pozzuole cement. Made from volcanic deposits, its durability increases the longer it is exposed to heat and cold, sun and rain. It appears to be impervious to decay. We continued on our way and came to the second bridge, still serviceable but not quite such a good example as the first, while the remaining three in the higher reaches of the valley could hardly be called bridges at all. They were fragmentary ruins; a partial span, crumbling eroded piers, broken walls and scattered stones.

There were many good walks in the region of Finale Borgo. It was possible to take various circular routes all beginning and ending at a café in the central piazza of the old town, the weather being still very warm and castle-hopping thirsty work a well placed café was essential. I say castle-hopping in a rather loose sense of the word, perhaps castle-crawling would be more apt as there were several scattered around the region most of which were perched on the summit of one steep hill or another.

One day at the start of an expedition we found ourselves mingling with a smartly dressed crowd in front of the Duomo and from the general buzz of anticipation we gathered that a bride and groom were scheduled to appear at any moment so we joined the spectators. The radiant couple emerged looking every inch the romantic prince and princess framed by the vast arch of the Gothic portal. They then underwent the customary bombardment of rice with a generous scattering of pasta which being the native staff of life was no doubt considered a particularly potent fertility symbol. However, the generous onslaught was not unopposed, The best man quickly produced a box from which the bride and groom sent retaliatory showers of sugared almonds into the crowd. The sweets were individually wrapped in snowy organdie that flew into the air like so many butterflies and to watch the elegant wedding party leaping and scrambling in pursuit of the sweets was very funny indeed. But the minute a shower of missiles came within our range, English reserve was forgotten and we leapt and scrabbled with the best of them. Whenever we scored a catch there were cheers and bravos, without the slightest hint of resentment of our presence or participation and we continued on our walk with bulging pockets of trophies.

It was not until later that we looked at the episode in a rather more sober light and the cause of this volte-face was the sight that confronted our return. The party was now over and we re-crossed the square, deserted except for a lone figure clearing away the aftermath of the wedding battle, we were disturbed at the magnitude of the waste. The rice and pasta now lay in dusty heaps waiting to be shovelled into the waste bins, the glamour and fun and excitement overshadowed by this futile debris. Common sense told us that it could do nothing to help the starving millions who are dying every day for the want of a bowl of rice but the evidence of waste was painful all the same. I found myself wondering why synthetic fertility symbols, plastic rice perhaps, would not do just as well as the real thing but maybe someone has already preempted me with this idea.

The many towns along the narrow coastal shelf all offered interesting diversion, each one quite distinctive from its neighbour though separated by only a river or a rocky promontory. There was a snag though to these otherwise pleasant explorations, the congested condition of the only interconnecting road to serve the coastal towns. Consequently, we took to using public transport, either the trains or busses both of which were extremely good systems. We did try driving into Genoa once and arrived so frazzled we were unable to make much of the trip and decided to use the bus next time.

Genoa is a city of great contrast: luxurious palaces rub shoulders with humble alley dwellings, the Centro Storico is overshadowed by glossy offices and stores, yet all combines to an integral whole. The port is the oldest and largest in Italy and is protected by an incredible three mile long breakwater. Naturally it is an important stopping place for passenger liners and also offers services for pleasure boats, naval repairs, and an immense tonnage of merchant shipping. I have always found ports interesting, and to be in close proximity to a major seaport where commerce at all levels is executed and with world-wide merchandise passing in and out is particularly fascinating but there was more to Genoa than mariners and commerce. It is not nicknamed the Superb for nothing, for from its dominant position at the apex of the Gulf of Genoa the city forms a great ampitheatre littered with innumerable palaces of great nobility. One of our objectives was to visit at least one gallery of art without having a fixed preference, and out of the hat came the Palazzo Spinola. We wandered inside on impulse and enjoyed a most unusual tour that turned out to be a private viewing. In a city where great art collections are so abundant, it is not surprising that some of them have their quiet times and our impulse coincided with one of them. Ceremoniously we were escorted from one grand room to another by a most dignified attendant whose demeanour was a combination of discreet bodyguard and superior butler. The rooms housed a fine collection of Flemish and Italian Renaissance paintings and these were displayed alongside furnishings in contemporaneous style, magnificent Venetian chandeliers and huge ornate mirrors. The frescoed ceilings were by Tavarona; a finishing touch of rare and sumptuous elegance, and all this exquisite luxury seemed to be for our sole benefit. It was a delightful experience and thoroughly appreciated.

Afterwards we succeeded in losing ourselves in the convolutions of the old quarter in which many small traders such as bakers, cobblers, tailors, carpenters and others worked at their various skills in small open premises. Customers actually watched their suit being made or their bread baked. It was so enthralling that we forgot the time and arrived at St. Lawrence Cathedral just as it was closing for the afternoon and had to be content with the outside. It was not easy to view satisfactorily because of its position facing a smallish square that was solidly parked-up with cars. If you stood back to admire the façade you were liable to be run over in the melee to snatch a vacant spot so it was close range or nothing. I am therefore only able to recall individual details but nothing of the whole, the steps flanked by a pair of 19C lions that guard the approach, a fine rose window, and a rather curious 13C sundial in the form of a knife-grinding angel similar to one we had seen at Chartres.

By this time we were ravenous and found a waterfront café, a cavernous sort of place. The tables were small, mostly set for one or at the most two, and the diners appeared to be mostly local workers, either in overalls or office 'uniforms'. From this we guessed that the food would be both reasonably priced and worth eating, and so it was. We ate a simple pasta meal but with a sauce that was new to us, a Genovese speciality called pesto made from a mixture of pine nuts, olive oil, basil, garlic and parmesan. It has since become a popular feature of our diet. We also had a sweet almond pastry, and as we were not in the car, we were able to indulge in an excellent dry wine, which was most likely responsible for what followed. Resuming the itinerary we plunged back into the 'Centro Storico' en route for via Garibaldi, a street of many stately palaces, and so came across the remnants of a market. Most of the stalls had either packed up or were in the process of doing so, but in one corner a book stall seemed in no hurry to call it a day and inevitably we could not pass without 'just looking' I swear that books give off a magnetic quality that is impossible to evade, it is an addiction. Anyway, it proved to be an introduction to the thrill of bargaining, Rolof Beny's photographs of Italy, a superb souvenir, came down in price little by little from £20 to £10. In triumph we carried away the prize regardless of a considerable weight and a not inconsiderable distance to cover before the bus was due to take us back to base. The burden was suffered gladly and is a valuable addition to our travel library.

Soon after this, we realised a long-standing ambition to visit Sicily. It must have been early October and the easier autumn weather offered good prospects for the thousand-mile drive. To add interest and cut out the tiresome return drive, it was decided to sail back from Palermo to Genoa by Sicily Ferries and we took the precaution of making an advanced booking.

There was still a pressing need for economy with inflation beginning to creep up and our income fixed but we refused to bow to restrictions of our travel programme. Resources were therefore husbanded by eating simple picnic meals and sleeping in the car, our diminutive motorhome, but we had reckoned without the autumnal scourge of mosquitoes. At the end of day one we reached Ansedonia, 290 demanding but very attractive miles, and soon found what appeared to be an idyllic camping place in a wild olive grove overlooking the sea. It was quite close to a newly excavated Roman site on a cliff-top and by the fading evening light we walked amongst the ruins. The dry undergrowth glowed with patches of yellow crocus, saffron, and delicate wild cyclamen, swallows and swifts circled high overhead, and cicadas filled the silence with their insistent chirping. It couldn't have been more romantic. Then with darkness the idyll ended as the enemy moved in and launched their attack. A hasty retreat to the car gave no relief as the beasts had already infiltrated and proceeded to give us one hell of a night. We must have killed scores as we slapped ourselves and wherever one landed in the car but reinforcements continued to arrive throughout those long sleepless hours. At first light, we made our get-away, making for the nearest Lido to wash away the torments of the night.

The day was only marginally better, for as soon as the heat of the sun began to make itself felt, the itch-scratch cycle was set in motion. The insects had done a thorough job leaving very little unmarked flesh and the contents of the first-aid kit was hardly adequate to deal with the situation. When we tried to supplement the insect bite cream at a small town pharmacia, all we could find was an aerosol spray deterrent, a shutting of the stable door after the horse had gone.

The Etruscan excavations of Tarquinia were on our itinerary but because of the crack-of-dawn flight our arrival was far too early, the place was still locked up but we fared better at Ostia. After a drive of about a hundred miles, the turnstiles were just beginning to click and once again, we enjoyed a lovely fresh early viewing. The history of Rome's ancient port is strange. It prospered and declined within a relatively short period of time, defeated and depopulated not by the usual force of arms but by the scourge of swamp fever for which Rome and its environs were notorious. Founded in the 4th century BC it prospered and grew to over 100,000 inhabitants becoming the trading port and naval base of Rome when the Empire was at its zenith. The decline began under Constantine in the 4th century AD greatly exacerbated by malaria and the silting up of its harbour.

Excavation has only been seriously undertaken since 1909, consequently the ruins are in pretty good shape not having crumbled too much although we did see signs of work being done with cement to aid their preservation. It was pleasant walking through the tree lined avenues that bisected the ruins, the silence broken only by the sigh of the wind in pine and cypress. We only met one other tourist in the hour we spent in Ostia Antica, a young American who was methodically working his way round all the historic sites in Italy in the true Jamesian manner. We would have welcomed a little more of his company but I suspect that our flea-bitten appearance put him off and who could blame him, we must have looked rather unsavoury. Anyway he hurried away and presumably sprayed himself with disinfectant as soon as possible to immunise himself against our dreadful, no doubt contagious, disease.

We took to the Autostrada for awhile to gobble up the built up commercial area in the region of Salerno but once past there and almost at Maratea we made our way back onto the minor roads hoping to find a village shop where we might buy food for supper. It was after sunset and almost dark when we came to a dour looking place by the name of Buonabitacolo; a misnomer if ever there was one. In the half-shadow that precedes total darkness, it looked anything but a 'good living place'. It was the most dejected of villages but having said that, there was a shop of sorts and we found all we needed for a more than adequate evening meal. Amongst the piled disorder that littered the bare, and probably none too clean board floor we found the best Lambrusco we ever tasted, and there was good bread, cheese, ham and grapes, a veritable banquet in fact. A further short drive brought us to a quiet hill road where we found a generous pull-off to make camp for the night and there were no mosquitoes. We dined and slept like lords that night.

We made the usual early start, always one of my favourite times when the unknown stretches ahead full of mystery. This should be the last stage down to Reggio di Calabria and the short ferry to Messina; tonight we would sleep on Trinacria – meaning triangle – well named by the Ancient Greeks. It was a lovely morning, full of wonderful sights and sounds and scents as the sun rose above the monochromatic landscape of mountain and valley. Here were the most outrageously perched villages without any visible means of access, the woods by the roadside were fringed with golden rod and other fragrant autumn flowering plants, and the birds seemed to have mistaken the seasons, giving us a dawn chorus that you would normally expect to hear in the spring. The Contadini, both men and women were already at work in the fields, but the only other vehicle encountered for many miles was an ox-drawn farm wagon. It was drawn by two beautiful beasts the colour of fresh cream who lumbered patiently along towing a load of maize and on top of this high load perched the wagoner. We stopped to give them room to pass, the road being barely wide enough for the two of us, and took the opportunity to snap the ensemble for our records. This woke the driver from his morning torpor and elicited cheery greetings and thanks, a nice exchange that left a pleasant glow in its wake.

Although these insignificant encounters appear to be given greater prominence that they deserve, it is a simple fact that cheerful courtesy freely given to a foreigner can assume the hand of friendship. It helps to alleviate the loneliness of the alien, or so it was in our case, and 'buon giorno' given and received made the day seem brighter.

The rare beauty of the quiet mountain passes could not last indefinitely, and after a while we found our road precipitated once more into arterial coastal conditions. Being so far south and away from the mainstream tourist resorts we assumed, mistakenly as it happens, that here would be found that rarity, unspoilt fishing communities. Even here the simple style of life was a thing of the past, the coast was a mess of transition having lost its identity of rurality but not yet acquired the veneer of a finished watering place. It can only be a matter of time before the entire Mediterranean coast becomes a hideous concrete shelf from which all natural beauty has been eliminated.

A few dozen miles of building sites and 'heavy plant' type traffic and we rebelled and looked for an upland track. Anything to escape from the horrors of the developers. At last, a vineyard entrance with enough rough ground on which to park suggested a much needed lunch break. As the last of the Buonabitacolo ham was demolished, a Piaggio piled high with a harvest of purple grapes destined for the vendemmia pulled up alongside the Lancia. Expecting to be warned off his land we prepared to apologise and leave quietly but to our surprise the driver, and a boy of about twelve got out of their vehicle simply to wish us 'buon appetito'. The man proceeded to rummage about amongst his grapes and gestured to us that we should join him and when we complied, he presented us each with a magnificent bunch of grapes. We were quite overcome by this spontaneous generosity and for an instant hardly knew how to react but as the man and boy were about to drive away I suddenly remembered that our 'canteen' contained a packet of chocolate biscuits and gave these to the youngster. He beamed and shook hands in the most delightfully grown up manner before we parted. After two such encounters in one day, we came to the conclusion that the southern Italians must be a social-minded and most amiable race that the new-look coastal developments had not yet disenchanted.

The final stretch of the journey down to the ferry at Villa Giovanni was an improvement that took us through orange and lemon groves of intensely dark foliage contrasting with the brilliance of the ripening fruit. The towns and villages were in the same state of flux here in southern Calabria with building in progress everywhere and roads disintegrating under the stress. Despite the influx of new property, the general impression was one of backwardness and the struggle for survival. The washing hung limply from strings looped against house fronts unprotected from the dust of passing traffic, and another peculiar custom was the way in which butchers displayed the meat. Suspended from iron hooks outside the shops were joints of meat, strings of sausages, even whole carcasses all exposed like the laundry to the prevalent dust and probably to flies too. It is possible that refrigeration was still a luxury in the Mezzo Giorno, or maybe that old habits die-hard.

The towns might have looked dejected but not the people. The overall image was one of vivacity, of attractive confident looks even in the poorest surroundings. And this same physical trait extended right across into Sicily where many of the towns showed signs of squalor that seemed not to effect the appearance of those who lived amongst it. Striking physical beauty was the rule rather than the exception.

As we joined the queue for the Messina ferry we were pounced on by a lad of about nine or ten who proceeded to spray our windscreen from a squeezy bottle before asking us would we like it to be cleaned. These embryonic businessmen were everywhere, and as our view was obscured by his mother's washing-up liquid, we gave him the go-ahead. He attacked the screen vigorously with his squeegee taking all of thirty seconds and promptly held out his hand. He drove a hard bargain refusing to give change for our proffered note of 1,000 lira, which was not a bad rate of pay for no more than five minutes work.

The Messina straits are an incredible shade of blue shot with green, like the iridescent plumage of a peacock, and it had the effect late in the day of draining colour from the land as we approached. Messina and the mountains behind looked coldly grey and undistinguished, an impression that close contact when we landed did nothing to dispel. The waterfront traffic was wild. The Italian driving was sedate compared to this and we got away from the city as quickly as possible. It wasn't only that we were tired after three days on the road and inadequate sleep, not to mention the mosquito bites, the driving really was bad. It lacked all discipline and from the incredible number of cars with mutilated bodywork, it was fairly obvious that drivers were not averse to leaning on anything that gets in the way. Consequently, we got out of the way before Fulvia should join their ranks. We passed through several nondescript villages along what appeared to us as a rather desolate coast on the way to Taormina, but it was the usual story, traveller's block when all the world looks grim and you wish yourself anywhere but where you are. Why make these journeys that end so feebly you ask yourself, 'wouldn't it be better to stay peacefully at home and not roam the world' says Cervantes but then the Zen in me echoes 'To travel is to be alive but to get somewhere is to be dead' So that is the answer, keep travelling but never arrive.

However here we were and once again in need of a place to bed down for the night but there was no seclusion to be found so for the first time we had to resort to an orthodox campsite. It was at Giardin Naxos, a lovely name at any rate, and we were also able to take advantage of 'mod cons', showers and a hot meal in a reasonable caféteria. I was still obsessed by the fear of mosquitoes and in the humid evening I was sure there were some lurking about, but we managed to sleep unmolested.

A new day and predictably the negative mood had evaporated like dew in the rising sun, to be replaced by buoyant optimism. The enthusiasm to explore Sicily was back in full force and Taormina was the first objective. The town lay directly above the campsite at an altitude of 675ft and is approached by way of a steep twisting road. Ten minutes and we looked out over the sea from the splendid natural balcony whereon Taormina stands and under normal conditions we should have seen the great volcano of Etna overshadowing the town but on this day it was obscured by cloud. The indications were hopeful for a sighting later on, as the sky was perfectly clear to the south; it was just an early heat haze.

It was rather surprising to find the streets free of traffic with plenty of parking space and with fulvia comfortably ensconced we set off to explore Taormina on foot. Its flower filled streets certainly lived up to the well-established reputation of great beauty that so many travellers have extolled in so many books. Every nook and cranny, every balcony and terrace overflowed with colour and the scent was almost overpowering. It was opening time for shops with great sweeping and washing of pavements before putting out the day's display of goods. Sweet smelling bread was being delivered in huge baskets, Etna bread, the best in the world, or so claim the Sicilians. We were inclined to agree with their boast; four days of existing on bread for almost every meal must be ample recommendation, for that is what ensued.

We came across a curious link with our island home on the wall above a doorway. The symbol of three legs, the Manx national symbol that is part of their flag indeed part of their history, I believe there is a motto belonging to it which goes 'Whichever way you throw me I'll still stand'. We were baffled by its appearance here, so far from home but at a later date, the mystery was made clear. The badge that we took for granted as being unique to the Isle of Man, was in fact derived from the Greek Cross or 'gammadion', a cross with equal arms each bent at right angles, and this has been used from ancient times by many different cultures. Sicily may have incorporated the three legs during the Norman period, 11th and 12th centuries, and one theory as to how and when it reached Mann is that it came through Alexander King of Scotland who won the island from the Vikings in 1266. He had previously attended the English Court during negotiations by Edmund, son of Henry the third, for the throne of Sicily. Edmund adopted the badge of the Mediterranean island and it is thought that when Alexander came into possession of the Isle of Mann he may possibly have brought it with him to replace the old Viking ship emblem.

Leaving our moment of nostalgia behind, at nine o'clock we climbed the steep approach steps to the Greek theatre, a legacy of the Hellenic period, and once inside climbed again to the upper terraces, to the 'best seats'. Here is the finest view of all in a city of great vistas, where the ancient proscenium frames an extensive littoral and, on this occasion, the lower slopes of Etna whose cone was still shrouded in mist. The Greeks certainly knew how to use a dramatic situation to advantage, to enhance their own dramas, and this must be one of their finest. To attend a performance during the season of classical plays would be an enviable experience.

On returning to reclaim the Lancia, we found the street had filled up and two battered old Fiats had taken advantage of our absence to make themselves rather too familiar. They were literally bumper to bumper. Now we had to practice the Sicilian method of extricating ourselves, a little surreptitious leaning and edging and gradually we were clear, and strangely enough, the exercise met with the approval of onlookers who had watched our dilemma with interest.

A short hop along the coast brought us to Fiumefreddo and from here we turned inland to skirt Etna to find at last the country we had anticipated, a landscape of gentle umber hills, pinewoods, citrus, olive and almond groves. As the road climbed it bisected a river of lava still smouldering from an eruption earlier in the year. We could smell the acrid sulphur fumes and saw partially engulfed farm buildings that appeared to be still occupied. This was D.H.Lawrence's 'Brilliant intolerable lava, walking like a royal snake down the mountain to the sea'.

Along the Adrano road, there are wonderful views of the Simeto valley, an incredibly fertile mass of orange and lemon trees that contrast sharply with the upper lava-scarred slopes. Suddenly, the cloud that had clung so obstinately to the cone drifted away and there at last was the infamous plume of smoke, innocent now as it coiled gracefully from the snow covered peak. It was a strangely moving moment, exciting too as we wondered how it must feel to live in the shadow of this perceptively docile monster that presently purred but could roar at any time and with such devastating results. Because of the recent activity, the ascent of Etna and an excursion to the crater was temporarily suspended, but we had been close and felt the power, it was enough.

We gradually worked across country, missing the right-hand corner of the triangle in order to reach Agrigento at the end of that day. The distance was something in the region of 100 kilometres but the roads being empty of all but a few mule-mounted peasants made it a very easy drive. Nothing like the drudgery of coast-road travel. Sicilian landscape at this season is bleached to pale ochre by summer's fiery heat, but the previous week had seen the first autumn rain and already the earth was responding. An almost imperceptible green was beginning to cover bare ground and roadside banks glowed with a mosaic of tiny flowers: miniature marigolds, daisies, speedwell, and sky-blue campanulas so short as to be practically stem-less as though long imprisonment made them impatient to burst into bloom the minute the rains drew their heads above ground. It was a kind of spring, a false spring overshadowed with the hints of autumnal melancholy.

An increase in agricultural activity indicated our approach to civilisation, to the commerce of fast growth for quick return. Plasti-culture was not quite so commonplace then as it is now and from a distance the black plastic covered acres had us flummoxed, from a distance they gleamed in an attractive liquid way but at close quarters it was a squalid disfigurement of rurality. Another strange nuance in the landscape that had us guessing for a while was a distant glass mountain. A hillside that glittered with a thousand irregular facets that turned out to be a bottle dump; a glacier of smashed wine bottles.

It was our intention that night to indulge in the luxury of an hotel, a real bed with a real bath, and had it not been for the anticipation for such necessities, we might easily have been put off Agrigento by the shoddiness of the approach. The tenemented northside was a mess of refuse and rubble, derelict buildings and abandoned cars, but we persevered doggedly through the dross until it was eventually left behind and we reached an oasis. It was the Piazza Roma, a garden square of beautiful mature lime trees at the heart of a crazy merry-go-round of unceasing traffic.

The pleasure of the Romany-like existence in the wilds were many and varied but finding a room with a bed and bath after four days on the road was almost ecstatic. The spirit of adventure is fine, it adds an extra piquant dimension to existence but that doesn't mean that a good night's sleep and a little hygiene should be scoffed at, nor for that matter the exchange of eating rough for a good plate of well cooked fish at a nicely set table. The appreciation is simply all the greater.

On the way to the little fish restaurant, we had almost been deafened by the evening roost of a thousand sparrows in the piazza trees but as we walked back, 'home' to the albergo there were different, yet equally insistent, noises abroad. It was indistinct to begin with, impossible to identify, but the volume increased to explode into fever pitch when we entered the square in which our hotel was situated. And this cacophony that filled the air at ten in the evening was simply children at play. Children of all ages, on bikes, or roller skates, or kicking footballs, - whatever the activity the principal ingredient was a loud voice, everyone seemed to be shouting and if they had not looked so amiable, one would have been misled into suspecting a smouldering riot. It was to this lullaby that we finally fell asleep. When it all simmered down and the young of Agrigento went to their own beds to recharge their batteries heaven alone knew, but we certainly didn't.

At dawn, it was the birds again who sounded the reveille to be augmented by the clatter of street sounds. The wheels of a new day were early in motion and it was useless to lie long in bed in the face of such get-up-and-go, much as another hour or so of oblivion was desired. At seven, we were up, dressed, packed and checked out of the hotel and shrugging off the dregs of sleep over coffee at the inevitable bar before embarking on the main object of this journey. To visit the renowned Valley of Temples.

Once out in the fresh newly minted day we were grateful to the sparrows and their dawn squabbles. Had it not been for them we might have wasted a perfect morning and missed the amazing sight of Doric Temples at sunrise. We followed the Strada Panoramica, a well named road that leads down the south face of Agrigento's hill, and from here you see a magnificent spectacle of the entire Valley of Temples, distant but perfectly unobstructed. We could hardly wait to have a closer look and were not disappointed.

Leaving the car all on its own in a vast open car park we set off on foot, once again the early start giving us the wonderful advantage of being the sole occupants of a historic site. This was even better than Pompeii and Ostia as there were no turnstiles, no gates to bar a timely approach and we really did have the place to ourselves. In the low sunlight the stone was the colour of warm honey, just fractionally darker than the baked earth, Almond trees and prickly pears grew in profusion amongst fallen pillars and pedestals and broken pediments and the gnarled old olive trees seemed as old as the site itself. At one point we found ourselves looking back beyond a magnificent Temple of Concord to the town, the southerly aspect that is so different from the awful back-alley approach we had made on the previous day. This was the Fair Akragas of the Greeks, situated on a hill that overlooks the great temples and the not far distant sea.

Almost two hours flew by like lightning as we browsed amongst the ancient stones, marvelling at form and shape and enormous dimensions. Concord, Dioscures, Hercules, Juno and Jupiter, what names to conjure with, what golden legends are recalled from way back in the mists of memory. The Temple of Jupiter is impressive for its size, although largely in ruins, and this is underlined by the reconstruction of one of many telemones, (columns in the form of male figures) that once supported its entablature and now lies prostrate, the 25 foot Gigante. It was not only the stones that made an impact. When I stopped for a breather, resting on what could have been a fallen architrave, I spotted two buzzards circling overhead. Lizards were everywhere, scuttling under our feet to disappear into crannies with the rasping sound of dead leaves and once I almost stepped onto a well-camouflaged snake that was sunning itself in the dust. I don't know which of us was the more startled as it streaked away to insinuate itself into a sliver of a crevice. And the butterflies filled the air with colour and dance, a kaleidoscope of constantly moving rainbow hues.

When we returned to the car park, we found several other vehicles were keeping the Lancia company and yet there had been no sign of their respective owners. We must all have been well dispersed. It was time now to leave Agrigento and we again struck inland driving north across the sparsely populated interior towards Cefalu. It was hot but pleasantly so for now the sun was in decline and need no longer be regarded as an enemy to be shunned as is the case throughout the summer months. On the contrary, this was a season to be savoured before the winter brought the other extreme of discomfort, cold winds and rain. We had no trouble finding a suitable picnic place, it was possible to stop anywhere by the roadside and be undisturbed by passing traffic. There just wasn't any. A la Omar Khyam we had our loaf of bread and flask of wine beneath the bough of a fragrant eucalyptus and felt there could be no finer way of living.

For a hundred miles this ideal state continued until we descended to the Gulf of Termini Imerese and the town of the same name, a nasty but necessary oil terminal. A few miles more in an easterly direction and the industrial sprawl was left behind to be replaced by a most striking sight, Cefalu at the foot of a solitary but very high cliff. What makes it particularly impressive is the position of its splendid Romanesque cathedral at the highest point of the town backed by the huge rocky promontory. As we drew closer, it was the excellent bathing beach that attracted our attention. Sightseeing could wait. A swim in that cobalt water must be superior to other paler seas we imagined and in a way, it was. It was certainly a wonderful antidote to many days spent cooped up in the little Fulvia.

Refreshed by our lovely long swim, we set off to look at that magnificent cathedral and arrived with the entrance of a wedding party. The beautiful people were more entrancing than ever in their wedding finery, and the floral display almost outshone, but not quite, the glittering 12C Byzantine mosaic in the central apse. It would be difficult to imagine a more elegant setting for a wedding, but it lacked one essential component, music. Where were the organ solos that accompany the arrival of guests, where the majestic voluntary of the bride's entrance and afterwards, the triumphal procession of bride and her groom? There is no music at all at these Latin nuptials, only words and for all the pomp and solemnity it seems incomplete when deprived of the joy of music.

We again slept under the stars that night, high on a hill-road outside the town, but enthusiasm for the freedom of wild camping was on the wane. I was losing my nerve. It may have been a stray thought that we were in Mafia country, iso-lated from family and friends who had no idea where we were; we could disappear without trace. Fear certainly got me in its grip that night making me oblivious to the beauty that sur-rounded us, the full moon coming up over the tree tops and myriad's of stars covering the sky. The night seemed endless and by morning, I had made a firm resolution that this would be the last night of car camping.

The morning was spent exploring the old streets of fishermen's cottages and small shops where we restocked the picnic supplies in readiness for the journey by sea to Genoa. Quite unexpectedly we came upon an Arab laundry, a relic of the Saracen period of the 9th/10th century. It was in the form of a semi-subterranean chamber housing several stone troughs that were fed by a channelled steam, and each trough had its own scrubbing slab. It was so well preserved it could still have been utilised.

At mid-day we left for Palermo hoping to have some time for at least a cursory look around before embarking for Genoa. How unprepared we were for the shock of the suicidal driving that we met on entering the city. There was no disci-pline whatever on the overcrowded multi-lane highways and the slightest gap between you and the car in front was an open invitation for some crazy cut and thrust driver who might overtake without warning from either side, or from any of the four lanes. To apply the brakes was courting disaster from behind, as there was sure to be another maniac waiting to pounce. It was a nightmare that I would not wish to repeat.

In view of this it was hardly surprising that we missed the turn off for the Sicily Ferries departure quay and were soon hopelessly adrift, drawn on inexorably along a seeming-ly endless waterfront. We wasted the best part of an hour manoeuvring back onto the eastbound carriageway and locat-ing our ferry, and almost missed this a second time due to inadequate signposts. This left little time to explore before the official boarding time and in any case the enthusiasm had cooled during that nerve shattering drive, nevertheless we left the car on the quay front and went off to see what we could on foot.

This was better but still not without problems. To cross that seething mass of kamikaze drivers was to take your life in your hands but somehow or other we made it to the other side and found a group of fishmonger's stalls. These were unlike anything we had come across before, including the comprehensive Chioggia fish market. It was not so much the variety here but the size of their wares. There seemed to be a competition amongst the onlookers at guessing the weight of the huge monsters that lay on the slabs. This was no crowd of trifling dilettantes, their manners were those of the confident connoisseur and at the nub of their interest, after elbowing a way through, we saw an immense swordfish. It was probably at the centre of a wager because while we watched the animal was weighed from a huge spring balance and turned the scales at something over 900 kilos – almost a ton. After this, we went in search of a quiet shady spot to eat a very late picnic lunch but the only garden we found was locked. It turned out to be a very neglected Villa Giulia, a place where it is reputed that Goethe used to walk.

Back at the ferry, departure time came and passed while we waited along with about half a dozen other cars on the hot, dusty and extremely dreary quayside. Meanwhile the lorries were being loaded aboard the triple-stern-doored Freccia Blu. These great doors swallowed up a seemingly endless stream of long-loads destined for all parts of Europe and we began to wonder if the boarding officer had forgotten our existence. This august person was a formidable German lady with the figure of an all-in wrestler and an authority to match. It required great temerity to approach her with even the mildest of enquiries let alone a hint of complaint.

The wait was alleviated to some degree by sharing our grumbles with fellow sufferers, who to our great relief were compatriots. They were Eric and Julia Watson who came from Guildford and had been staying with a married daughter in Cefalu. Their stories of driving in Palermo outdid our own limited experience. Once, when harassed beyond endurance, they abandoned their car in midstream so to speak, found a telephone and begged their Sicilian doctor son-in-law to come to their rescue. It was mutually agreed that there could be no worse place to drive that Palermo and if there was, we had no wish to go there.

Once the boat sailed the frustration of being three hours behind schedule was quickly forgotten and we settled down to enjoy the twenty-four hour crossing. It was flat calm and the time passed pleasantly in the company of our new-found travel companions. After weeks of struggling to make oneself understood in our still rudimentary Italian it was a joy to relax and converse in our own language. We reached 'home' in Finale Ligure at eight in the evening, seven days from setting out and only one of those seven nights had been spent in a bed. We were very tired.

Soon after the Sicily trip the weather turned quite chilly and the nights positively cold. It became obvious that with the onset of winter our north facing, tile-floored, unheated rooms would be altogether unsuitable for a lengthy stay. It was imperative that alternative accommodation should be found, but rather than restricting our move within the area we decided to opt for something completely different. Spain for instance. For us at this time Spain was 'terra incognito', we had never set foot in the Peninsula so there was the double incentive of finding a temperate winter climate and exploring new ground.

Before making a positive decision however a minor crisis arose and the plan was temporarily shelved. The now two week old mosquito bites showed no sign of healing on me although Eric's had completely cleared and it became obvious that infection had set in. Form E111 now proved its worth. We duly called at the appropriate office, filled in forms, and were then at liberty to consult a local GP. It was an interesting experience. There was no receptionist, no appointment, just a simple waiting room on the second floor of an apartment block in which about half a dozen patients waited their turn. All newcomers were greeted with polite 'Buona sera' and a welcoming smile. It might have been a social gathering, a few neighbours meeting for coffee. When my turn came the consultation overcame the language block and I was soon on my way to a chemist, to return a few minutes later to the surgery armed with tablets, cream and an injection, the latter to be administered by the doctor. All this was given completely free of charge and in a most sympathetic spirit and within twenty-four hours the infection had gone, cleared up completely and I was free of the scratch/itch cycle at last.

Now the plans for change went ahead with a preliminary three day foray via the south of France, the Pyrenees and into the corner of Spain that is Catalonia. We were delighted with what we found and in no time at all we had reserved an apartment in a small industrial town of Palamos about seventy miles north of Barcelona. November the first was to be moving day, an exciting prospect of yet another phase in our voyage of discovery, a phase that was to present Italy with a serious rival for our allegiance.

Chapter Eight

Discovering Catalonia

'Now is the winter of our discontent made glorious summer by this sun of Spain'

Shakespeare.

It was raining when we left Finale Ligure at the unearthly hour of seven a.m. bitingly cold and not yet light. If this was a foretaste of Riviera winter weather, it certainly softened the blow of leaving. Even so the departure was not without a touch of melancholy, the regret of parting from a friend, but this was tempered by the stimulus of a new liaison ahead, and as with all new ventures we were well aware of the snags that must be overcome. There was the language problem for a start. Having made some headway with Italian it must be put aside and a new set of practical phrases mastered and likewise a new monetary system and fresh shopping techniques dealt with. All in all the mood was a mixture of 'what have we let ourselves in for now' and 'no regrets, a new world is there for our gratification'.

The weather grew steadily worse. The transition from darkness to daylight could hardly be detected and the rain continued to fall in blinding sheets, making driving conditions intolerable. We were tense with anxiety at the thought of 400 miles of monotonous windscreen wipers flicking to and fro and minimal visibility. The normally glamorous Riviera autostrada that takes you leaping across chasms and tunnelling through mountains, past San Remo, Monte Carlo, Nice and Cannes, was an absolute washout. It was hard to equate this journey with the one of only two weeks ago with its wide views of terracotta and white villages cascading down to the brink of steep cliffs above a flawless blue sea, and the palm groves and flowering shrubs. Now all that could be seen was rain, mist, and the car ahead.

A break came as we crossed the Rhone valley somewhere in the region of the Camargue. The rain stopped and the mist began to lift, slowly at first trailing ragged veils of sullen grey, and then it was gone. There was still a heavy ceiling of cloud but at least the landscape had reappeared and incredibly, we found ourselves overlooking an inland lagoon crowded with flamingoes. Their bright pink plumage stood out sharply against the silvery-grey water, the first bright spot in that day of unmitigated gloom. We stopped of course and out came binoculars to watch in close-up the stately interplay of their movements, take-off and resettlement, an ever-changing tapestry of pink and grey. The short stop extended to a tea break, we were reluctant to leave the rare display for such a chance may never occur again, but there was still a long way to go, and the rain came again.

The crossing from France to Spain was by way of La Junquera, a border town that has become a cross between a marshalling yard for lorries and a duty-free depot. For more than a mile east and west of the custom post lorries waited to have their credentials checked, parked and double-parked in every available space. It was an impressive sight and a reminder that these giants of the road have more than traffic conditions to deal with, there are also the complicated logistics of transferring their loads across frontiers from one end of Europe to the other.

Besides being one of Europe's principal commercial crossroads, La Junquera was another great crossing point in our programme of events. By the simple act of negotiating that mile-long ravine formed by great pantechnicons, we bid goodbye to the Italian adventure and approached a new one in Spain. Initially we went there in search of a temperate winter climate but we were to find much more, a vast and infinitely variable country and warm-hearted people who gave us a courteous welcome as guests of their country.

Estartit had been the base for the original foray. Besides the pertinence of its name for a new project, it also turned up trumps with the most fantastic Hostal in terms of comfort and value for money that we ever experienced. So naturally, this was where we stayed on that first night, the day before we were due to claim the Palamos apartment. Hostal Santa Anna welcomed us back and we ate our first paella and slept the sleep of exhaustion. The 400-mile drive in heavy rain had taken its toll and Santa Anna's luxury was greatly appreciated. I say luxury but in fact the room, bathroom, and breakfast was 1,600 pesetas, slightly less at that time than £8.

The morning of November 1st we were away early, impatient to establish the new home, and as this was All Saint's day it was likely that mid-day would be closing time, the rest of the day being holiday. There was a lot to do before close down. However, we made good time, covering the intervening 40 miles very easily on quiet uncluttered roads, the first notable difference from Italy. We collected the keys to Calle Enrique Vinke with a remarkable lack of formality, the ladies in the agency office refusing to accept the payment of rent until 'manana'. Today we close early for the holiday they said; we will see you in the morning. This was extreme trust we were quite overwhelmed. Here we had the keys to a beautiful seafront apartment without any elaborate procedures, there was to be no inventory, no rules, just a firm belief in our honesty. We could scarcely believe our good fortune.

That time was quite dreamlike. The unpacking was lingered over as though we knew this would last. The home-making equipment was arranged, it is quite surprising how a few books and photographs, a vase of flowers and the odd cushion or two can transform an anonymous furnished flat into something personal. Within days it was home. We tried to resist the temptation to pick up memorabilia, but inevitably, a few artefacts crept into our basic travel kit. A Majolica vase from Albisola, a teapot and a pair of china cups and saucers from Finale, candlesticks from somewhere else until gradually the apartments reflected the course of our travels. Unlike any previous residence occupied since the start of our peregrinations, this one had everything, position, space, adequate furniture and equipment and central heating, although this last item was rarely needed. It was also unusual in having wood block floors instead of the usual tile or marble, and the furniture was good solid stuff that required amazonian effort to move it about. Two bathrooms and a model kitchen completed the picture except that is for the magnificent south facing balcony. We spent hours on that balcony, dined there, worked there, or simply leant on the railing watching the world go by on the paseo below. The Palamos paseo at that time was a wide tree-lined avenue of hard packed sand, the trees mostly pollarded planes that formed a corridor of leafy 'umbrellas' in the summer but now presented a picture of so many naked (and knobbly) arms raised in supplication. It took some time to get used to this drastic regimented treatment but we soon realised the logic that governed this custom. A tree left to itself in the Mediterranean climate grows to immense height giving inadequate shade, a commodity as necessary as food and drink in the heat of summer, consequently every available shrub, vine and tree is made use of for this purpose.

Beyond the paseo lay a wide sweep of golden sand and the sea. Palamos is situated at the eastern end of a wide bay, the western arm reaching out in a long mountainous section almost as far as the region's capitol Sant Feliu de Guixols. At night, after the sun had dropped behind the mountains, they came alive with thousands of twinkling lights, an indication of urbanisation that was invisible during daylight.

We have often been asked what made us chose Palamos out of all the many glorious resorts of the Costa Brava. The setting apart, it could not by any stretch of the imagination claim to be other that an attractive working town, and that is probably the crux of the matter. Its small engineering and cork manufactories gave our northern spirits a familiar ethos, it seemed to be fundamentally true, a real place as opposed to the glamorous façade of purely tourist resorts.

In addition to light industry, it was also the centre of a sizeable fishing fleet and with harbour facilities for the occasional large tramp or lesser cruise ship. At one time, its sheltered position and exceptional deep-water dock had given the town a larger share of commercial trade but with the advent of containerisation, it lost out to the greater facilities of city ports. However, it still maintained a certain amount of trade. Glazed tiles arrived from the Middle East, which struck us as a coals to Newcastle analogy considering that the pottery centre of La Bisbals was only ten miles along the road. We also watched the unloading of great cargoes of hardwoods from the rain forests of South America. The mass destruction of tropical forests was only just filtering through the channels of the general consciousness and the sight of so many fallen giants waiting to be transferred to the sawmills was an intensely thought provoking concern.

A lighter and quite stimulating sight was the morning exodus of the fishing fleet. About forty boats would leave their berths in the inner harbour, make their way round the long arm of the breakwater to gather in fleet formation below the lighthouse. On the stroke of seven the diesel engines roared into life with an overwhelming rush of sound and they were off, the daily fishermen's Grand Prix. The heart stirring throb of the combined engines and the spectacle of the little working boats sailing into the path of the rising sun was worth getting up early for, and there were invariably a few aficionados to see them off.

The return was also a popular feature though not quite so spectacular, as the boats were now strung out and would come singly or in pairs. Few can resist the mystique of watching the unloading of the day's catch, the free entertainment of amazing shapes and forms from the minute to the monstrous. We enjoyed the atmosphere of the auction in the 'Lonja' the fish exchange, it was a constant mystery how traders and fishermen could make anything of the cryptic grunts of the auctioneer but somehow the fish changed hands and reached the shops so the system apparently does work.

Another characteristic of Palamos was the street produce market that took place daily and occupied the full length of the central shopping street and a section of the harbour road. It attracted traders large and small from a wide area, some little old ladies having nothing but a few potatoes or tomatoes or figs from their gardens, which might bring a meagre supplement to a poor pension. The larger stalls were brilliant, a staggering profusion of colour, a feast of scents of fruit both commonplace and exotic. It was all so lively, a sort of social focal point in the day and we rarely missed a visit even when we needed nothing.

Besides the day to day routine, there was often the additional spice of special events, sardana dances on the paseo whenever a feast day occurred, the International dinghy races at Christmas, Carnival week, and the Easter celebration. It was all new to us and highly entertaining. The Catalan ring dance was one of the most frequent events and was probably my favourite. My first introduction to the sardanas was one Sunday when we happened to be at home. At 12 o'clock the sound of music - a reedy not quite tuned music that was foreign to our ears - drifted up from below drawing us, as music habitually does, to a vantage point, our balcony ring-side seat. The 'cobla' or small wind and drum band first played an introduction and then the rings formed, small to begin with but growing as each new dancer joined in, with hands held high, bodies straight verging on stiff, and all the skill in the footwork. It was not a select performance by a group of specialists but a universal pastime and all ages took part from very young to senior citizens and if I could have summoned up the nerve I too could have taken a place in the stately circle but I never did. It was not to everyone's taste. I have seen it described as 'faun-like capering in prancing circles' while a Madrid friend considered it stiff, poker-faced, lacking the vigour and dash of Flamenco, but to me it has a hypnotic quality of restrained energy and calm precision.

We had been quite prepared to celebrate Christmas in a quiet way, it was one of the sacrifices set against the many dividends of the exercise, but then at the eleventh hour two chance meetings changed the outlook considerably. The first breakthrough came on the 22nd when greetings were exchanged with two ladies from a neighbouring flat as we all came in from the street together. This was not the first time that we had passed the time of day but it had never gone beyond that so it came as a surprise when the senora detained us. She introduced herself as Senora Garcia and her companion as tante Joanna and then we were lost. For some reason the conversation proceeded in German until tante Joanna grasped the fact that we were English and haltingly made us understand that we were being invited to tea the following afternoon. The senora's daughter Montse was due to arrive home from Austria to spend the holiday with her mother and apparently could speak English 'very good', and Mum had taken this initiative to show off her daughter's skill. We only hoped that she wouldn't mind two strangers thrust upon her on the very first day of her holiday. As it turned out we became good friends but it could quite easily have been otherwise. We were astonished to receive such an invitation knowing how unusual it is for a Spaniard to open his home to a foreigner or even a casual friend, it being the custom to entertain in restaurants. And we were complete strangers.

Later the same day in the local food-store, 'Superstop', I happened to overhear English being spoken in an unmistakable Scots accent and without stopping to consider I pounced. This was the first of many instant friendships made between compatriots when it becomes imperative to strike quickly; it's a case of now or never. There is no time to waste on the tentative approach and within minutes names, addresses, and invitations had been exchanged.

Alex Denovan, a retired RAF navigator who was recovering from a recent stroke, and his wife Eileen were wintering at La Fosca, a holiday village satellite of Palamos, to escape from the snows of their home in Dunkeld, Perthshire. Life suddenly took on another dimension, instead of sitting brooding over Christmas festivals that were gone, other doors were opening and we could share goodwill with Spain and the 'old country'.

We attended the Spanish tea party with a mixture of apprehension and pleasurable anticipation. We were greeted by senora Garcia and ushered into a handsome sitting room to be closely inspected by two dogs, the senora's golden spaniel Damma and a large though fortunately friendly cross-bred alsatian belonging to tante Joanna that answered to the name of Yute. After an exchange of formal chit-chat conversation ground to a halt and still the daughter Montse had not appeared. The tea was brought in, and then milk, and lemon and sugar all in relays and suddenly, like a whirlwind from heaven the missing Montse rushed in. She had apparently been sent out to buy cakes, on the assumption that all English people took tea and cream cakes at four o'clock without exception.

During the tea ceremony while we dutifully consumed massive sticky cakes and weak chilly tea, conversation was almost equally chilly. It is not easy to appear erudite or to sparkle with wit when dealing with such unmanageable confections as the Spaniards produce for the sweet-toothed. I suppose we were all holding back at first, Montse in particular being almost silent and for a while I suspected that she resented being bulldozed into this meeting. But it wasn't resentment; it was simply shyness and once her initial reserve thawed it was replaced by the other extreme, an ebullient enthusiasm certainly equal to, if not greater than, her mothers. She had an insatiable desire to learn all about the English way of life and was happy to tell all she could about theirs, so that by the time we came to leave we were the best of friends. We asked about the name Montse that we had noticed repeatedly in Palamos and indeed was also the senora's Christian name. It was we were told a diminutive of Montserrat, the patron saint of Catalunya, and it was the custom throughout the entire province to name ones first-born daughter after their saint.

Before the party broke up we learned that Montse was a music student studying piano at Salzburg, and without a moment's hesitation she offered Eric the use of her baby-grand when he acknowledged that he shared her love of the piano. This gesture was enthusiastically taken up by Eric and made the Palamos episode quite exceptional. He had missed music making more than he cared to admit and had certainly not expected to be presented with such an opportunity under present circumstances.

This was the first of many similar get-togethers although we did manage to dissuade the senora from buying cakes, especially when we learned that they did not normally eat sweet things themselves, in fact the tea ceremony was purely for our benefit. Under normal circumstances, 4 o'clock would be just about the end of their lunchtime which made the gesture of their acknowledgement of the English afternoon tea quite remarkable.

On Christmas Eve, there was a concert of festive music given by a visiting choir in the local church of Santa Maria del Mar. It was a warm evening, and even warmer in the packed church so that Jingle Bells and The Holly and the Ivy, already curious in the foreign tongue and harsh local style, seemed almost outlandish in the sub-tropical atmosphere. The choir though not exactly a threat to 'Kings' was totally dedicated and bounding with vigour and the congregation loved it. Each item commanded their whole attention until the final phrase and then there was an explosion of rapturous applause and at the end of the published programme the choir were not allowed to leave until well past midnight with an endless number of encores delivered to the satisfaction of the insatiable audience.

The ceremony of paseo-ing was in full flood on a warm and sunny Xmas day, warm enough for dresses and shirt-sleeve order and the colourful crowd were dressed accordingly. We joined the holiday throng and met George and Elizabeth. No, not our one time king and queen, but a holidaying German couple with whom we struck up a casual acquaintance. We never ceased to marvel at the ease with which these encounters happened, to develop not infrequently into lasting friendships unhampered by any language barriers.

Back at Enrique Vincke the celebration lunch of corn-fed chicken and a cheap (£1) bottle of champagne Spanish style was taken on the balcony and lingered over most of the afternoon in the true national fashion. San Esteban (Boxing

Day) was shared in a similar way with Eileen and Alex Denovan. We talked and talked as though our lives depended on it through lunch and tea and on to sundowners on the balcony, and what a sundown it was. Those December sunsets over the sea at Palamos were incredible. Each one was different, each compulsive viewing; each one built up to a spectacular climax before fading into obscurity. The whole spectrum of colours were there, sometimes to rest on ephemeral wisps of cloud, or great banks of cumulus, the sky might be pink, flame or blood red all to be reflected in the sea. Turner would have enjoyed a field day capturing those excessive sky and seascapes.

Life reverted to normal immediately after the two-day festival of Xmas and St. Stephens until Epiphany when Spain celebrates the Magi's homage to the Christ child with the festa of Los Tres Reyes. It is observed principally as the day of giving presents to the children and depending upon the prosperity or otherwise of the location is celebrated with varying degrees of refinement. Costumed Magi might be splendid or homespun, their mounts anything from mules to camels, from jeeps to tractors. In Palamos the Kings arrived by sea in fishing boats, making a triumphant entry into the Plaza Major on a tractor, a modified edition of the original version but in perfect keeping with the seafaring ambience. Excitement reached fever pitch amongst the children as the names were called and the gifts distributed (by courtesy of parents of course). The following morning was the grand parade of the families showing off their new acquisitions: tiny tots in racing cars, motor bikes and tractors, with plenty of frustrated tears from the drivers and eager exhortations from enthusiastic fathers. The girls were less prone to trouble with highly florescent pink or blue doll's prams while the older children terrorised the esplanade on bikes, roller skates or skateboards. It was almost as dangerous as crossing Piccadilly Circus in the rush hour and quite as noisy.

The good weather continued but nights were colder and so was the sea, so we gave up swimming for the time being. But the walking was superb. Miles of good paths followed the rugged coastline - the Costa Brava - revealing hidden coves and golden beaches enclosed by rocky promontories to which stone pines clung, growing almost to the water's edge. There were days when the wind whipped up the waters of the bay and instantly the sailboard fraternity appeared in force to transform the usually placid scene into action packed arena. The first ripple on the water and they converged on the bay like swarms of highly coloured butterflies. This was the popular wind, the llevieg that comes from the west but when the tramontana blew down from the north, it was quite another story. The fishermen hated this wind and not a boat stirred from its berth. It smelt of snow and ice and shrivelled the soul not to mention the sandblasting received by the body. It was a time to lie low and wait, like the fishermen, for a wind-change. We were surprised at how cold these days could be and how inadequate the dress of the majority. The most common defence was a jacket or woolly cardigan clutched under the chin in a futile attempt to keep the bitter wind at bay. Warm overcoats or even anoraks were quite rarely seen although we were certainly glad of ours.

Spring came in with a rush. Wild flowers seemed to explode into brilliant life, a multifarious collection that was a joy to my amateur botanising nature, and the scent of mimosa and almond filled the air. The short winter was over and as the fishing boats resumed the daily ritual of the Grand Prix, we made plans to resume the exploration of Catalonia. Barcelona and Girona were top of the list but we also had it in mind to visit the Salvador Dali museum at Figueras and the Greco Roman site at Empurias. It promised to be a full and interesting programme.

The distance to Barcelona is seventy miles, two hours by comfortable service bus. Having learnt from experience in Genoa that cars and sightseeing in cities are incompatible, we did not hesitate to use public service transport. We found the Catalan capital a city of widely contrasting elements, teeming suburbs of stark high-rise tenements, relieved of absolute squalor by pot plants on balconies, a splash of red geraniums lit by whatever sunlight might penetrate the concrete chasms.

Suburbs gave way to wide tree-lined avenues that bisect the city in long magnificent sweeps, one being almost six miles in length. Then the Gothic Quarter gives another aspect with its warren of dark streets some of them dating back to the 13C, and the absolute juxtaposition of this is the surrealist architecture of Antonio Gaudi. It would be futile to attempt to describe the treasures of Spain's second largest city, for as I write it has become a world-renowned showplace in the final stages of preparations for the 1992 Olympic Games. Already through media coverage, there can be few people unfamiliar with Gaudi's Church of the Holy Family, left incomplete in 1926 when Gaudi was run over by a tram. Work is apparently going ahead to finish the building in quite another original style which adds yet another contrast to my list.

We ate our lunch in a delightful green and peaceful public park before plunging into the old quarter in search of the cathedral. This was no easy matter, it is a well kept secret, but we made it eventually only to lose ourselves even more completely on the way out. We followed one blind alley after another going further and further astray until we found ourselves in the heart of the red-light district. Well, we had heard of houses of ill repute but had not expected to include a tour of such a street in our itinerary. Pathetic travesties of beauty, mini-skirted and painted, lounged in the red glow of open doorways. Once the penny dropped and I realised where we were a peculiar mixture of fear and embarrassment gave new impetus to my tired feet and I set off at a ridiculous pace to escape from watchful painted eyes. Eric was meanwhile busy trying to sort out our route from a rather inadequate town plan and had noticed nothing singular in our surroundings, that is until my bid for the four minute mile, when it became incumbent on him to give chase. It was funny in retrospect, once back amongst the cosy respectable flower sellers of the Ramblas, that breathless rush of an agitated middle-aged woman hotly pursued by an equally anxious middle-aged man running such an incongruous gauntlet.

The remaining time was spent more profitably in the Picasso museum in the fine 14C Aguilar Palace, but we were not sorry to take our seats for the return bus journey, sight-seeing is an exhausting occupation.

Girona, the provincial capitol, is smaller than Barcelona but no less interesting. It enjoys a particularly privileged site at the juncture of two rivers, the Ter and the Onyar, the old town occupying a promontory with the modern city spreading below on both sides of the river. The tightly enclosed historic centre is perfect for exploratory strolling. There is a lot to see in a compact area, and quiet corners to rest and contemplate when the need arises. The cathedral was a must of course being particularly notable for its unusual construction of a single aisle which makes it outstandingly spacious and light.

Personal impressions of the city, whose foundations go back to pre Christian times are of a light, well cared for, unassertive sort of place. Yet it has every reason to be proud of its fine buildings, parks tree-lined avenues and general sense of well being. The public park of Devesa has extensive woods of fantastically tall trees, living illustrations of what happens when they are left unpruned. From one of several bridges spanning the Onyar there is a good view of unusual tiered houses that appear to rise directly from the river which reflects row upon row of vari-coloured windows and shutters. We loved the small but attractive Rambla with its flowering trees and pavement cafes, stylish without being intimidating.

The first time we went into Girona was a Sunday in February and in spite of sun, we were surprisingly cold. We had grown used to warmer coastal conditions and here at only 25 miles inland there was a considerable drop in temperature. This was also our first visit to the cathedral and we timed it well, Mass was about to commence, and the warm church with the prospect of some good singing and organ music tempted us to remain as observers.

We were doomed to disappointment. The ecclesiastical ritual was imposing with its army of priests and acolytes, its veritable smoke screen of incense, but of music there was nothing to speak of. The 'choir' consisted of two quite elderly tremolo precentors, and the organist, if he woke up in time, played an introductory chord for the occasional mournful chant. Eric, ever the optimist, was sure that there would at least be an outgoing voluntary and we had a quiet bet on it. I won. We walked out to the sound of many feet clattering on the stone paving and I duly claimed my winnings - 25 pesetas!

After a bowl of hot though unidentifiable soup and a dish of fried fish, the 'Menu del dia' at an unpretentious café on the Rambla, we felt warm enough to continue the exploratory ramble and so found the 'Banyos Arabs'. It was an interesting late 12C building with a particularly striking frigidarium, an area with a pool surrounded by columns and lit by an unusual lantern. More to our taste on this particularly frigid day were the tepidarium, warm room, the hypocaust, steam baths, and best of all the caladarium or hot room. The effect was all in the mind of course as the baths were no longer in use except as a museum.

The third excursion on our hypothetical shopping list was something quite different, the Neapolis and Roman town at Empuries. It is situated on the coast in the opposite direction to Barcelona, a much quieter and very beautiful area to reach which we drove north through fruit-farming country. It was a lovely day, the birds sang with the joy of spring and the wild flowers were at their best, a good day for such an excursion. The ticket barriers when we arrived were closed, the place was not due to open officially until Easter but it did not matter in the least. Apart from the museum, everything was accessible and to our advantage for apart from a few isolated winter wanderers like ourselves, the place was deserted.

There may have been a shortage of homo sapiens but whereas Agrigento had been populous with butterflies, Empurias was a haven for the feathered vertebrates. Flocks of goldfinches and crested tits, firecrests, serins and those pompous mini-morning-suited sardinian warblers. The electric-blue flash of a kingfisher down by the ornamental pool almost stole the show but was beaten by a wing tip into second place by our first hoopoe. As we turned a corner, there he was, strutting along the path a mere metre ahead of us. In a flash, his alarm crest shot up and he was off with his characteristic open shut wing movement that we came to know so well.

It wasn't all bird watching. We did study the cyclopean walls, colonnades, domus peristyles, and mosaic pavements. The ruins cover a considerable area and date back more than two thousand years, one restricted site containing a piling up of different periods of developments. In the 6C BC the first settlement was founded on what then was a small offshore island that is now joined to the mainland and occupied by the village of Sant Marti d'Empuries. A century or so later a new town was established on the mainland as a Greek trading post and this situation existed until 49BC. Then the Romans moved in. Caesar installed a colony as a port of entry for Roman influence in the Peninsula, which in its turn succumbed to the Moors in the 8C. As a port, it declined when superseded by the new city of Tarraco (now Tarragona). A small beach close by the ruins still retains traces of its seafaring history, with solid looking remains of a Roman jetty or breakwater a few yards out in the bay.

And so to Figueras, birthplace of Salvador Dali. The weather had taken a nose-dive, it was a damp misty morning evocative of England in November rather than a Spanish spring but the objective being the Dali collection, the drizzle could be ignored. The museum was a very appropriate setting for the eccentric artist's dramatic creations being a converted theatre, and it was rumoured at the time that the old man himself lived there in his own 'ivory tower'. A for-taste of things to come assails the visitor before setting foot inside the building, a trio of ponderous 'thinkers' enthroned on pedestals of stacked worn out lorry tyres - 'the apotheosis of Catalan philosophy' - a 30ft high tower of defunct television sets - 20C totem pole - and decorating the theatre's cornice, nude shop-window dummies alternate with giant gilt eggs, presumably representing fertility symbols.

Inside one must be prepared for anything. The artist's fertile satirical imagination had designed a kind of artistic fun-house, often macabre, sometimes amusing, serious work

137

contiguous with bizarre, but always entertaining. One might walk into an open mouth, lascivious painted lips framing the portals of a door, a gracious formal salon with an outrageous ceiling, a simulation of the frescos in the Sistine chapel carried out with effective irony. For two hours we were shocked, moved, amused, amazed, and never for a moment bored. Dali's sense of the ridiculous went hand in hand with his artistic genius and search for beauty. He was a controversial character and often labelled a charlatan, but surely there is a place for the vivacious and the absurd that looks askance at humanity and a world inclined to take itself too seriously.

Carnival fell during the first week in March. The streets and shops of Palamos were decorated with bunting and everyone from bank managers to street sweepers were disguised by most striking costumes, the emphasis being on the comedy characters Harlequin and Columbine. But the highlight came with the pre Lent processions. Groups representing towns and villages of the region vied with one another for supremacy and the result was a display of considerable panache, taking into consideration the relatively limited resources of these small communities. Enthusiasm overflowed into an intoxicating barrage of noise. Brass bands, whistles, a beating of drums and tambourines, maintaining an incessant pulse far into the night.

As spring advanced and days grew longer and warmer, the end of our allotted six month period in Palamos loomed disconcertingly large. The final weeks raced by as though someone had thrown the 'fast forward' switch, but there was still time enough for new experiences. The most significant by far was a meeting that was to lead us on to a particularly rewarding third incursion later that year, into the Deep South, into, 'real' Spain. We met Raymond Lockyer on a walk near the fishing village of Calella; a pretty enclosed cove of white houses and pine clad hillsides. He was a retired architect and practising artist, in self-imposed exile for the winter months from his Cotswold home and his wife, because by his own admission, he hated the cold whereas his wife loved the winter activities of their village and could not stand heat. So for five months they agreed to go their separate ways. His wife's loss was our gain as he was admirable company being a great raconteur, and from past experience he was able to give us a few pointers to the most unexploited regions in southern Spain. It was from Raymond that we heard of Almunecar, but that chapter is yet to be written.

Easter, heralded by Palm Sunday was late that year, being at the end of April, and with it came the first heat wave. The Palm Sunday service was celebrated outside in the church square. It is an attractive ritual of the carrying of palm fronds, intricately woven and decorated with red and yellow striped ribbons the Catalan colours. The children are the chief participants with the women behind them bearing laurel branches, and the whole town turns out in new spring outfits, a symbolic bidding goodbye to winter and welcome spring. After church there was the habitual strolling on the paseo that on this special day was a veritable and most elegant fashion parade. I had a rather nasty moment when returning from an early walk. Being unaware of the Easter Parade I walked slap into the middle of it wearing jeans and trainers, like gatecrashing a party unsuitable dressed.

The good weather brought crowds of visitors from the cities for the Easter weekend but there were no further signs of extraordinary ceremonies, the Holy Week processions being a speciality of Andalusia. Here the shops were full of chocolate eggs and many elaborate confections in the form of animals, horse-drawn carriages and even castles, and instead of hot-cross buns, they eat small sugary doughnuts called bunjelas. For a couple of days the beaches filled with sun-worshippers and luxury yachts were aired but by Monday it was back to normal. And then we too packed our bags and bid Palamos adios, but with many a backward glance, 'hasta la vista' was the prevailing mood.

Chapter Nine

From Palamos to Almunecar

'For whereso'er I turn my ravished eyes, gay gilded scenes and shining prospects rise'
Joseph Addison.

I should perhaps at this point give an explanation for the annual trek back to northern latitudes. It was purely a matter of economics. Our total income from the initial investment taken out in 1982 brought us about £80 per week, and on this we could live and travel reasonably comfortably as long as we restricted activities to the off season, that is from about October to the end of April. The exodus was forced by the summer influx of holiday crowds and consequent massive increase in prices.

We survived the interim period in subsistence standard English 'rooms' mitigated by a round of visits to family and friends. Britain basked in sub-tropical conditions that summer of 1984 which helped to soften the enforced period of vacuity, yet even so we itched to be back on the road again.

For the first time we knew in advance where we were going and actually had a new home waiting. The plan was to spend the autumn in Palamos renewing friendships and making the most of the available sun, sea, and sand, prior to setting out in search of another new episode. Meanwhile home was to be Enrique Vincke again.

The route south was down through southwest France crossing the Pyrenees by the Roncesvalle Pass and then came the revelation of the Spanish interior. Vast open spaces, ever changing earth and rock formations and colours, and an immense sky under which my being seemed to expand and vitalise. We passed through Pamplona, stopped overnight at Huesca, continuing on through Llerida, by-passed Barcelona to arrive 'home' at the end of day four from leaving Thingwall on the Wirral.

Two weeks went by before social contacts could be renewed. The Garcia family were not back from their summer retreat in the mountains, the Denovans had not yet arrived, and Ray Lockyer had moved to another address which took a little detective work to locate. When Eileen and Alex did turn up in October they were full of the news that they had bought another flat further south at La Manga del Mar Menor near Cartegena. They had no intention of selling up at La Fosca, it was to be retained as a staging post, but the new place was to be the main winter residence and they were due to move down there in a week's time. It was disappointing to be losing them so soon but we were hardly in a position to complain in view of our own plans to go south before very long, and now the Denovan's new place might serve as a useful stop-over for that journey.

Meanwhile we all made good use of the intervening week to exchange news before their departure. Alex's weakness, one might even say addiction, for the acquisition of property had certainly not been trouble free. Their summer back home in Scotland had been almost entirely spent in clearing up the ravages of the previous winter when a severe freeze up had caused extensive damage to their Dunkeld house. It was a reminder that property was only an asset when fully occupied and well protected, otherwise it seemed to us to be nothing but a liability. We sympathised with their predicament but enjoyed the merest touch of complacency regarding our own rootless state.

It was not long after this that the Garcia's returned to Palamos and we quickly picked up the threads to be welcomed once again into their domestic routine. It was an enthusiastic reunion. The dogs went berserk; the ladies were equally excitable and talked nineteen to the dozen - in Spanish - until we managed to remind them that our

Spanish was only 'poco poco'. Montse explained that they were trying to convey the enthusiasm that they felt for the venue of their recent holiday. 'Ah! Cantallopes is so good, so tranquil, so beautiful, I wish to stay always there, I could teach pianoforte there' she bubbled with tremendous fervour. Cantallopes, it later transpired, is little more than a hamlet in the Pyrenees, tranquil yes but hardly a suitable venue to set up as a music teacher.

It was good to have our friendly neighbours back. We also had several interesting exchanges with senora Nuria, the lady who owned our apartment, and her French Consul husband, Roberto Palet Lebeau. Of all Spaniards with whom we attempted to converse they were the most successful. The senora in particular understood that it is necessary to speak slowly, enunciate clearly, and keep sentences short and in that way encounters were both profitable and a pleasure. Senor Palet Lebeau had first come to Spain to fight on the side of the republicans during the Civil War. After the war he stayed on and married Nuria and took on the consulship of France for the Costa Brava. The senora kept a huge Great Dane called Boris, an incredible animal who used to ride around in the back seat of a Renault 5, the most unlikely combination of dog and vehicle imaginable.

Once we had located Raymond Lockyer's new hideout, our social needs were amply catered for and there seemed no urgency to move on. Life was agreeable, and we were content for awhile to do nothing, comfort having blunted our resolve.

Two events stand out from this period of indolence. The first was a walk in the country that brought us to Cruilles, one of the old 'Conjunt Medieval' that abound in that part of the country. Many of the historic villages have been smartened up to attract tourists but this one was a little off the mainstream and had not yet received the treatment. It is all faded stucco, crumbling arches and pillars, and rusting wrought iron. A blank-faced church rubbed shoulders with a ruined watchtower, and narrow cobbled alleyways wandered from point to point in a most confusing manner. It was because of this air of neglect that we remember it with affection, that and a strange encounter with one of the elderly inhabitants.

A casual 'hola - buon dia' to a bright eyed little old lady taking the air beside her open door, elicited a most surprising response. She became extremely loquacious and with a 'pase usted, pase mi casa' we found ourselves ushered into her house. Although somewhat taken aback by the unexpectedness of the situation it was a great opportunity to see what lay behind the iron-grilled face of a Catalan rural home and we followed the diminutive black-clad figure with genuine curiosity. More extensive than outward appearances might suggest, one room let to another, all with identical roughcast whitewashed walls and well-worn terracotta tiled floors. Old photographs adorned one wall in the main room and one of these was brought to our attention - a carefully posed sepia representation of her parents, the father wearing the woollen long-berry that is still worn by shepherds today.

Furnishings throughout were simple, bordering on the spartan, but everything was spotlessly clean even to several immaculate ready made-up beds that made us wonder if it had once been a lodging house, or maybe still was and the old lady had an eye to business. But perhaps not. When she demonstrated the wonders of running water in the kitchen and bathroom we suspected that here lay the mystery of our presence. A newly bricked up well in the rear courtyard was further proof that it was the phenomenon of modern technology that she was longing to show off to an appreciative audience so what could we do but exclaim appropriately. All this was conducted with barely a word of comprehension, Catalan requiring even greater sign language than our limited Spanish but we managed, and it seemed obvious that the interlude had pleased our hostess who waved us off with smiles and a volley of adios and hasta luegos.

The second incident also gave an insight into the ordinary everyday life of rural Catalunia. It began with a meeting in the middle of a noisy crowd of market shoppers with senora Garcia. She proceeded in her usual polyglot way to express a 'wonderbar idee', she never could remember that we were English not German, - why should we not go to Cantallopes on Christmas Eve - was the gist of her exciting idea. As they had no car we could be the taxi, and she knew a very special place where we could eat as her guests. The suggestion appealed to us and arrangements went ahead although we were rather concerned about numbers as the Lancia's back seat would only take two and that with difficulty. However, we need not have worried as tante Joanna had made other arrangements and would take care of the dogs.

At first sight the undistinguished huddle of stone buildings that called itself Cantallopes made us wonder what all the fuss was about. Was this the epitome of young Montse's dreams? Her genius loci? It could not boast one architectural gem, no quaint corners with beguiling café-bars, but neither were there traffic jams, or neon lights, or discos. Also on the positive side was its unique position and herein lay the secret of its charm. A green, south-facing valley, watered by a clear mountain stream and sheltered from the north by a forested ridge of the Pyrenees. It is a sea-facing, sunny, flower-filled oasis: roses, violets, ox-eyed daises, marigolds and bougainvillaea all jumbled happily together regardless of season in a riot of colour and scent. We began to understand.

A friend of the senoras was to join our lunch party, the first of many surprises in a surprising day. Meanwhile there was some shopping to do and a guided tour to be undertaken under the auspices of our young friend who was dying to show us some favourite haunts; a hump-backed bridge over a waterfall, the ivy covered church (little more than a chapel) hidden away in a tiny cobble-stoned plaza, and finally their summer apartment that looked out over the sun-filled valley and distant sea. Yes, we could definitely understand and were rapidly falling victims ourselves to the subtle magic.

The shop from which we purchased our Christmas 'bird' was most discreet. We would not have noticed it without our guide. Plastic-ribbon curtaining successfully screened the emporium that supplied the community with its every need, food, clothing, hardware, toys, medicines, maybe even furniture, nothing would seem to be beyond their capabilities. To our friend this was the moment of homecoming. Montse apparently knew and loved everyone in the village and chattered enthusiastically to all comers until we began to fear that we could never prise her away. Our English constitutions told us it was lunchtime and as yet we had no idea where or when the promised meal would materialise.

At last Senor Cargols, the fifth member of our party was introduced to us and we learned that lunch was to be a 'little further on' and the senor would lead the way accompanied by the senora in his battered old fiat. If we thought Cantallopes was remote we had not, as they say, seen anything yet.

The road beyond the village petered out to a track resembling the bed of a dry watercourse. For seven kms that seemed more like seventy, we bumped and lurched agonisingly up through cork-oak woods to emerge at last in a high depression that gave an open view of fold upon fold of forested hills. In the middle distance one of the smaller hills was crowned by an enchanting castle seen against a background of high snow peaks, and round the next bend was our goal, the minute hamlet of Requesens.

It was really no more than a farm with scattered outbuildings and the restaurant was a wing of the main building. The entire complex had been built to supply the castle in its heyday but was now a rather precarious private enterprise. The exterior was unpromising but inside it was cosy enough with a table set for our party with green gingham cloths and bowls of marigolds. We were apparently the only expected clientele if the remaining bare tables were any indication and so it proved.

The meal was the next surprise. It began well enough with home baked bread and a simple salad of lettuce, tomatoes, olives and onions, to which we applied ourselves with razor sharp appetites. It was now after two, early for our

Spanish hosts but we never quite succeeded in adapting to their regime. With filled glasses we waited for the main course and when it came we could scarcely believe the evidence of our own eyes. The dish contained a heap of dark bony fragments of meat surrounded by a moat of oily liquid and unidentifiable fungus. The others set to with gusto and found no fault with it and we tentatively followed their example but it was hard going. When we asked what we were eating, the answer 'pato' failed to throw much light on the subject, but a charade of flapping wings and waddling and quacking solved the mystery. That old duck must have seen many summers before he landed in the pot. None too soon the offensive dish was taken away and replaced by a rather more enticing basket of giant clementines and a mixture of almonds and raisons. All was forgiven.

The wine continued to flow and the talk grew progressively more animated when the proprietor and his son joined in. Senor Cargols and the new arrival were old friends having grown up together during the civil War years, and with Montse fulfilling her usual role of interpreter they told stories of how fugitives and refugees had sheltered in these mountains on route for the French border. The boys acted as guides for both the escapees and those volunteers coming into Spain to join the International Brigade, the territory would have been difficult to navigate without help.

As we talked a wind began to blow with a weird moaning and whining that echoed round the old walls. It was the Tramontana they said, with rather less animation, and here we were at its very source. What is more it was to blow relentlessly for the next nine days.

Back in Palamos it was possible on our south facing sunny balcony to evade the cutting edge of the wind and we were even able to eat our Christmas lunch outside, but it wasn't much fun venturing abroad. Raymond came to dinner in the evening and in return for the home cooking he regaled us with an inexhaustible supply of amusing anecdotes. He was the society hostess's dream, the raconteur whose 'flashes of merriment were wont to set the table on a roar'

On the festival of San Estoban we were having drinks and tapas with the Garcia's, reviewing the trip to Cantallopes when the telephone rang and the message they received brought festivities to a sad end. We were all shocked to learn of the sudden death of senora Soley, their friend and our agent through whom we had leased our apartment. It was only two weeks since we had spoken to her, and now at the age of forty-two, her life had been snuffed out by a very rapid form of cancer. It was a reminder of human fallibility even in what one naively believes to be Utopia.

At last we were jerked into action and on New Years Eve wound up affairs in Palamos to make the journey down to Andalusia. We spent our last evening with Ray at his flat in Calella. His balcony overlooked a small pinewood, the round cushiony tops giving an illusion of a sea of softly billowing green waves. The actual sea lay beyond, a dark blue band of silk between the undulating treetops and the pale winter sky. We shared a bottle of champagne and waxed sentimental with more that a touch of melancholy, wondering why we were leaving such delights for yet another unknown quantity. But the old curiosity was at work and refused to be denied so with Raymond's advice to head south of Granada, in his opinion the only stretch of coast to compare with the one we had here, we parted, and sadly our paths have not crossed again.

The 700-mile drive along the N340 had, as far as I can recall, nothing to recommend it. The traffic was unrelenting, the coastal developments brash, and where the buildings ended the plastic forcing houses began. It was impossible to see much of the great cities such as Tarragona or Valencia on the way past, the traffic made sure we kept our eyes on the road, but there was a pleasant relief in the crossing of La Huerta, the great citrus groves of the latter region.

We made two overnight stops, the first at Sagunto close by the ancient hill-top citadel - not much chance to get any sleep there as we had inadvertently stopped on the fruit route, lorry loads of oranges passed our Hostal day and night. The second night we stayed with the Denovans at La

Manga. I don't know what we had expected but the reality was depressing to say the least. The strip of land two miles long by a quarter wide, a natural barrier dividing the open sea from an inland lagoon had been desecrated by tower blocks in the worst possible taste. It took a determined effort to imagine the area as it once was, a wild place of grass-grown sand dunes, glittering water and wild birds, perhaps even flamingos, but now this. However the welcome was warm enough and a good meal in their ebullient company followed by a comfortable night's sleep put us in a better frame of mind, but nothing, not even a perfect climate, could have persuaded Eric or myself to buy property in such a soul destroying urbanisation.

The landscape improved over the latter part of the journey especially with the crossing of the great desert region between Murcia and Almeria, by far the most unusual land-scape we had seen in all our travels. Apparently some scenes from the film Lawrence of Arabia had been shot in this area which is indicative of its wild environment. From Almeria the road followed the rugged coastline, twisting its way round every inbite and spur, every promontory and creek, with wonderful views of the high sierras revealed as we crossed the wide cultivated river estuary at Motril. Here the principal crop seemed to be sugar cane. An extensive 'prairie' of tall broad-bladed grass bisected by our wide road for a distance of about two miles, the only flat, straight section of the 80 miles from Almeria to Almunecar.

Twenty minutes more of further spectacular corniche driving brought us to journey's end, another cultivated val-ley, this one dark green with unrecognisable trees that reached inland as far as the eye could see. We discovered later that the area specialised in tropical fruits and the ones we couldn't identify were chirimoyas and avocados but more of that when we have established a new base. Unfortunately we had mistimed our arrival, one tends to forget what day it is on extended journeys, and it was now late in the day on a Saturday, an impossible time to plunge into house hunting, but by Monday afternoon we were taking up residence in our 'castle in Spain' and a whole new era began.

There was to be no unpacking and settling in that first day. The Fulvia's MGB identification label was once again the means of introduction to new friends. In this case it was fellow countryman Philip and Jeanne Marples who spotted our vehicle when we were filling up with petrol and immediately welcomed us and brought us into local society. It was Philip's 70th birthday and together with two friends they were planning a lunch party at a village inn up in the mountains, and asked us to join them. Although not fully recovered from the long haul down here, we could hardly refuse such a generous gesture.

The venue was at a village called Otivar, twelve miles inland up the old road to Granada, a twisting and badly surfaced road, but the scenery was glorious. This valley of the Chirimoyas was known as the Valle Tropical and the reason was obvious, it was dense with fruit exotics of all kinds from bananas to papayas, guava fruit to nicperros otherwise known as loquats. From the apples and pears of the north we had run the whole gamut, through Valencia's orange groves and Motril's sugar plantations to this incredibly prolific haven.

And so to Otivar and Franco Arcos' restaurant El Capricho. It was a basic no-nonsense venta, simply furnished even to paper tablecloths but the food was worth driving 700 miles for. Each couple was served with a whole spit-roasted chicken stuffed with garlic, apples and herbs, with an accompaniment of sauté potatoes, the usual Spanish salad, bread and a carafe of local wine, all for the equivalent of £5. There was nothing exotic in this menu yet everyone who ever sampled Franco's chicken dinners always returned again and again. It became a frequent habit of ours to spend a day walking the 'colinas' and 'barrancas' in this spectacular valley and finishing up at Franco's for a chicken or perhaps a rabbit. It was always 100% reliable.

Our new home was a small villa with a garden with a view, across rooftops and gardens, to old Almunecar, its castle and the sea beyond. It was all so beautiful that it seemed impossible, we must be dreaming because an income of £80 a week simply does not allow one to live in such ideal surroundings. So we told ourselves each morning as we looked out on that lovely, sunlit, floriferous world. The town was bigger than we had expected but had somehow managed to escape the worst excesses of tourist development. This may have been because of the distance of fifty miles to the nearest airport at Malaga, and eighty miles to that of Almeria. Consequently it had retained its Spanishness and its tourists came mainly from inland Spain.

The old town was quite different from those in the north. There they were for the most part stone coloured in various shades from grey to ochre but here they were startlingly white built in tightly packed layers, one above the other like giant bee-hives, generally crowned by either a castle or church. The shops were on the lowest level as also was the principal plaza and the ayuntamiento - a handsome town hall. There was a good produce market and with plenty of fresh fruit and vegetables available at extremely low prices we found it easy to keep within our budget and eat healthily.

By mid-January we had thoroughly charted Almunecar and its immediate environs, and now prepared to fulfil an ambition of long standing, to visit the three great Moorish cities of Granada, Cordoba, and Seville. The natural starting point was the Alhambra Palace at Granada, about two-hour's drive inland from Motril. Having no news, being cut off from media information, we were unaware that the whole of Europe was only just surfacing from the effects of freak blizzards that had actually come as close as forty miles, and, so we heard later, those valuable orange groves through which we had passed such a short time ago had been totally ruined. From a personal point of view, had we attempted this trip one week earlier, our route through the mountain pass to Granada would have been impassable.

Now it was clear and the heights of the Sierra Nevada with their freshly fallen snow were a magnificent sight against the rich blue of the southern sky. The lower slopes were covered with almond blossom in full flower reminding me of D H Lawrence and his 'See it come forth in blossom, From the snow-remembering heart, In long-nighted January' Thousands upon thousands of gnarled old almond trees transformed by the delicate blossom for their brief time of glory.

The recent cold spell must have deterred travellers for we found ourselves parking in comfort when we reached Alhambra, quite a unique situation in one of Europe's most famous tourist attractions. There were no queues, no crowds to distract or divide the attention. From the very beginning of our enterprise we seem to have been inordinately lucky with the spasmodic intrusions into tourist territory. It can't all have been due to good management.

Our progress was dreamlike, something of a fantasy from the Arabian Nights. The strongest, most vehement memory I retain is that of windows, magnificent windows with equally magnificent views. For as long as I can remember I have had a peculiar penchant for windows. When viewing a new house, or even visiting for the first time my instinct is to look outwards to check the surrounding aura, one can adapt interiors but a view is a fixture. So with the Alhambra I was in my element.

From the crenellations of the 9C Alcazabar the eyes are automatically drawn to the great mass of the glittering Sierra Nevada, - can there be any greater view from any other window in the world than that? In the Palace, every twist and turn reveals magnificently framed views, some external looking over gardens or the rooftops of Granada, and others inward looking onto cloistered gardens dripping with palm trees and fountains. Even the Generalife Gardens continue the theme of framed views, - media naranja arches revealing exquisite corners of courtyard or water-gardens. It was enough to satisfy the most voracious window addict. We have been back to the Alhambra on several occasions since that day, but the magic of first impact has never been recaptured, and in any case, conditions have never since been so impeccable.

Cordoba was the next objective and by mid-afternoon we set off to reduce the distance as much as possible before dark, to give us early access to the city on the following morning. The road led across undulating cultivated land, the fruitful vega of Granada. Mile upon mile of tended hillsides of orderly trees, olives, soft fruits and almonds that gave the country a peculiar plum-pudding appearance in an ever-recurring sequence of geometric patterns. The number of man-hours that had gone to produce such symmetry must have been phenomenal.

We stopped at Montilla, found a very reasonable Hostal and then explored the nightlife. By that I mean we joined the locals at a nearby bar to sample the Montilla wine. This was said to be the forerunner of sherry, for it was here that the 'solera' method of wine production was evolved and perfected, yet strangely enough it has never achieved the prestige of the Jerez sherries. We found it quite as good and considerably cheaper and have looked for the Montilla label ever since. Eric was impressed by the nonchalance of the drinkers. A workman might order wine, brandy, or beer, satisfy his immediate need and depart, leaving a glass part full to be poured down the drain. Imagine that in a pub back in the old country.

After a substantial breakfast of bread and Manchego cheese and large bowls of milky coffee we were set up for the second stage of the quest for the Moorish legacy. Cordoba stands on the right bank of the Guadalquivir River and owes its reputation partially to its long held position as capital of Muslim Spain during which the city enjoyed three centuries of peace. In the 10C a university was founded that achieved great renown, and it is also famous for maintaining a long tradition of leather and silver-filigree craft-work.

We parked the car on the left bank of the river and walked across the wide Puente Romano, an ideal approach that gives time to appreciate a sense of history. To the left of the bridge as we crossed we could see the remains of a large waterwheel also of Roman origin though probably much restored, and directly ahead, the walls of the great Mezquita-Catedral.

At the risk of being a bore, I have to state for the record that again the 'early bird' system worked like a dream. We did not catch the worm but we beat all other tourists to the post and even arrived before the ticket sellers. We entered by the Pardon Door alongside the Minaret, crossed the Court of Orange Trees with its symmetrical rows of fruit laden trees and into the Mosque by the Palm Door. And then we gasped, taken completely by surprise, for although we had seen plenty of photographs of the interior we were quite unprepared for the actuality, the forest of pillars topped by red and white arches that seem to go on for ever. The 16C Christian cathedral in the very heart of the Moorish arches did not please the reigning Emperor, Charles V who thought that something unique had been destroyed to build some-thing commonplace. For all its Gothic, Renaissance, and Italianate grandeur the sumptuousness simply looks out of place even a little vulgar beside the satisfying eternal quality of the surrounding Mosque, the original part of which dates back to the year 785.

It was almost 10 o'clock when we returned to present day Cordoba, slightly bemused and abstracted by what we had seen. It was a cool day of intermittent sun and cloud, just right for poking about and absorbing new territory, in fact so deeply absorbed that we were caught on the hop by a stranger who stopped and asked if we intended making a visit to the 14C Synagogue. It was one of only two still in existence in the country he told us and for some inexplicable reason we forgot our hard and fast rule to be independent of guides and found ourselves shadowing this man through the narrow streets of the Jewish quarter. Outside an insignifi-cant building we waited while a key was procured and were then allowed inside a small square room with a screened bal-cony to one side, to segregate the women of course, but was otherwise bare of furniture. The walls were decorated in grey and white Mudejar stucco, an arched alcove was painted blue with a scattering of gold stars, and several lanterns of Cordoba silver-filigree hung overhead, and that was all. It was mildly interesting but five minutes was quite enough and we turned to leave. Then came the crunch. Our self-appointed guide stood in the doorway and demanded 200 pesetas from each of us, the price we had paid for a morning in the Alhambra Palace. We offered him half of this but he was adamant and there was nothing to do but give way, but the experience strengthened our resolve not to succumb to solicitations of touts in the future.

We grumbled for awhile then put it down to experience and got on with the pleasures of wandering about the town that even in January is very beautiful. Our short tour culminated in Colt Square outside the posada described by Cervantes in Don Quixote, a necessary pilgrimage for two ardent fans of the famous Knight.

The road from Cordoba led through Ecija, popularly known as the furnace of Andalusia for its terrible scorching summer temperatures, but today it was green and pleasant, just the place to stop for our picnic lunch before pressing on to Seville. The city was not quite what I had expected. Influenced I suppose by scenes from Carmen and cosy descriptions of Cervantes and even early travellers tales. I imagined a city of guidebook proportions not this great humming business and industrial centre throbbing with traffic. It was a relief to find a quiet corner in which to park having safely negotiated several major road junctions, where groups of gypsy beggars defied death among the turmoil with appeals for alms.

Once across the Puente de Generalisimo and into old Seville, we found that the spirit of Carmen still lives, even to the Fabrica de Tabacos (now part of the University). We 'did' as many of the obligatory sights as half a day would permit, finishing at the Alcazares Reales, where thankfully we collapsed beside splashing fountains in the charming Moorish gardens. The Palace, another treasure house of Mudejar art, magnificent carved cedar-wood cupolas and ceilings, and a marvellous proliferation of 'media naranja' arches and carved stucco, occupied the greater portion of our allotted time. Of the Cathedral, we were inclined to agree with the verdict of the 15C chapter, 'a Cathedral so immense that everyone beholding it will take us for madmen'. It is a massive structure, the third largest after Rome's St Peters and London's St Pauls and when we crossed the threshold I had the feeling that I had bitten off too large a slice of sightseeing to digest properly at one go. A general impression would have to do, as there was no way in which I could have given the innumerable chapels more intense study, even given the inclination. Palaces and their gardens, and the mysterious grilled windows of ordinary houses, some with open doors giving glimpses of leafy inner courts, were what I found rewarding. But even these lost their appeal at the end of a long concentrated day of 'looking' at things. It was enough. It was time to return to the bougainvillaea-shaded terrace of 'Casa Nuestra' back in Almunecar.

The finale phase of the three cities tour reverted to the old Coates nightmare that dogged our early travels in Italy, that of not knowing how or when to stop. We were afraid of over-nighting in the city for economic reasons, besides being so footsore that the car seemed the best place to be. Confidently we left Seville with an hour of daylight in which we were sure to find a village inn along the road. Away from the city there was nothing but wide open vistas of freshly sprouting wheat-lands, and an occasional white-walled domain, a timeless sort of landscape that for awhile revived our flagging energy. The setting sun, low to our right, made an efflorescence of the landscape that threw into high relief a corral of highbred horses here or a ranch of fighting bulls there.

We passed through Jerez de la Frontera, past the great temples to Bachus: Harveys, Osbornes, Gonzalez Byass, Tio Pepe, Domecq, Crofts, each a household name, and each flamboyant palace doing its best to outshine its neighbour. And still we could not stop.

Our greatest regret, possibly for the entire three-year period of our European travels, was bypassing Cadiz. To have missed the city reputed to be the oldest in the world to be continuously inhabited under one name was quite a bitter disappointment in retrospect. But at the time there was nothing to be done about it. The road held us fast as it swept past along the Costa de la Luz and we lacked the will power to deviate. It was now quite dark; the Costa de la Oscura would have been a more fitting title for the winter coastline and our own depressed state. Somewhere along the way the impetus slowed enough to let us try for a room at a wayside hostal, but the bleak barrack-like place, reeking of damp and spiders, sent us off again with a last reserve of energy.

The rest is a vacuum of thrumming wheels and the passing glare of oncoming headlights that left a black void in their wake. Tarifa was another wasted opportunity, Europe's most southerly town and we skimmed through with barely a glance, but there was one small gleam of light in that evening of gloom. A cliff-top lay-by to the right of the road was an open invitation to stop and gather our scattered senses over a cup of tea. I set the kettle to boil and while we waited took a short walk to the cliff's edge. There across a narrow stretch of water, so close that it seemed no more that a stone's throw away, was the coast of Africa. Festoons of golden lights trimmed the edge of the Dark Continent leading to the mass of lights that we guessed must be Tangier. Straits of Gibraltar, Pillars of Hercules, the voyage of Ulysses, what visions that dark narrow channel conjured up from the past. It was an intensely moving moment that went some way to alleviate the pain that is the utmost degree of fatigue.

There was a moment when we considered spending the night on this mirador, but the arrival of a couple of other vehicles quickly scotched that idea and we drove into Algeciras determined to find a bed at whatever cost. Three times we applied the simple room-seeking formula and received negative response but at the last gasp, more dead than alive, the reply we longed for came up.

On entering the establishment, a tall dark narrow house, we were aware that it would not do to scrutinise the room, there was an insalubrious air that under any other circumstances would have put us off immediately, but we were past caring. When we reached the top of those interminable stairs there was no turning back regardless of a stuffy yet cold room and damp sheets on a narrow bed. We slept the sleep of the dead, for awhile that is, but the day had not finished with us yet. Noises in the night, amplified by the stone stairs and tiled walls had us abruptly awake and on edge. It was worse if anything than a certain night at Cortona during the journey through Italy when a domestic battle had disturbed the night hours. But this had a sinister flavour. Low moans, yells, dragging footsteps, retching sounds, - I discovered later that our room was next door to the bathroom - and between sleeping and waking, the nocturnal goings on appeared to continue throughout the night. It was sometime before the penny dropped and we realised that we had landed ourselves in a brothel. This was the seedy nightlife of the infamous gateway to Africa and had I not been so desperate for sleep the situation might have struck me as funny, - as in retrospect it did.

Our trusty Lancia seemed more than usually welcoming when we took off at a very early hour the next morning. We had no scruples about knocking up the landlord to check out after the treatment we had endured, but he seemed non too pleased and was apparently nursing a prodigious hangover. It was good to shake the cobwebs of that place off our heels. Gibraltar was soon in view, an impressive sight over the flat coastal plain, and we fancied the idea of breakfast on British soil and made our way to the frontier. But the Anglo-Spanish wrangle was a week off its peaceful solution and the problem of negotiating the inflexible customs post was too much to face on top of the ravages of the night. We had breakfast at La Linear at the wrong end of the narrow isthmus.

It was an uninspiring drive home. The only redeeming features along the whole of the concrete jungle coastline were the very occasional fishing ports that had somehow managed to escape the ineffable march of 'progress'

Almunecar seemed even more attractive by contrast with the 'Costa del Wimpy' and we settled down to enjoy its delights for the remaining weeks of the winter. Philip and Jeanne joined us for a meal and for a report on the Moorish expedition, and it was then that we heard the details of the widespread blizzards that came so close to the Costa del Sol. Palamos apparently had been hit very hard by the freak conditions less than a week after we left to travel south. For a week they suffered from frozen pipes followed by bursts, and there were deaths from inadequately heated homes and lack of warm clothing. They simply were not geared to dealing with such extreme conditions.

On the journey home to England we made a point of revisiting Palamos to see how our friends had fared during the crisis and were relieved to find them fit and well. Montse gave us a great send off with a real Spanish dinner, a very emotional affair, then it was 'Hasta la Vista'. Yes we would definitely return.

Chapter Ten

The Travel Bug Strikes Again

'All I seek, the heaven above, and the road below me'.
The Vagabond, R L Stevenson

Some time has passed since the foregoing chapters evolved. Since that last departure from Spain for home shores, we have, as was then predicted, returned time and time again. Consequently our knowledge of, and affinity with one particular area centred around Almunecar, has developed and grown stronger with increasing familiarity.

The first return, being the forerunner of many, is especially worthy of note as the one in which we established an extremely congenial base and made the first important contacts that were to lead to lasting friendships.

It began in much the same way as the original journey, with a visit to Norway in September 1987, to be followed by the long drive south through Denmark, Germany, Austria and into Italy to the Adriatic coast. Driving was infinitely more comfortable now with the extra space and power of the lately acquired Rover 2300. Instead of the five days it had taken in 1982, we did it in four and still without resorting to motorways, while using a slightly different route, we had the opportunity to absorb a little more of the countries through which we passed. With the September departure we had hoped to avoid arriving in Italy during the worst of the fierce summer heat but it was a futile hope. The Po delta where we planned to spend the first 2 weeks was steaming under a tropical heat wave. The Lido di Nazione south of Chioggia was quiet and well placed for forays into various intriguing towns with plenty of time, as we thought, for sea bathing in the Adriatic but this too turned out to be a futile hope. The sea was uninviting, muddy and shallow. We had failed to take into account its proximity to the great river estuary, and even the beach appeared to be suffering from the aftermath of storms with its generous consignment of driftwood and litter. The atmosphere, day after day was heavy with a yellowish dusty haze which the mosquitoes appeared to love, they were prolific. Had it not been for the valuable amenity of a swimming pool close to the apartment, we should not have survived one week let alone two. However to rest was essential before further journeys could be contemplated and meanwhile the diversion of interesting towns beckoned. There was Ravenna to be revisited while a visit to Pomposa Abbey was particularly rewarding with its distinguished 9C campanile. The fine view from the top was well worth the climb.

On September the 18th we left the Adriatic coast to drive, in thick mist, westwards to Finale Ligure, a distance of roughly 300 miles. Fortunately the mist cleared about an hour into the journey and we reached our destination before the letting agencies closed and promptly arranged possession of an apartment on a lush hillside site. It was very beautiful, exotic flowering trees and shrubs, extensive interesting views but it had one major drawback; it was situated halfway up a marble stairway of 500 steps. The car had to be parked at the summit and all luggage or shopping had to be carried down 250 infernal steps, or up depending on which direction we approached. Not quite my idea of a stairway to paradise.

The weather continued hot but at least here the sea was delightful, crystal clear and a wonderful easy temperature making a daily swim an absolute must. We spent a month on the Scalinata delle Rose during which time many of our previous Ligurian haunts were rediscovered, some to fall short of remembered glories while others gave fresh satisfaction. The most outstanding was a second look at Venice, a journey we made by train. When I came across the details of this trip from a diary of the period, I was at first mystified by the timing. Why had we not gone into Venice from Lido di Nazione instead of making this not inconsiderable journey just three weeks later? The reason of course became obvious when I remembered how intolerable the heat and humidity had been, how extremely lethargic we were as a result, conditions inexpedient to sightseeing.

We took the night train, 9:30 from Finale Ligure arriving in Venice in the small hours at 4:30am, not the most auspicious of moments at which to begin exploring this unique city. We were obliged to wait for daylight and meanwhile to find a sheltered place to mitigate the pre-dawn chill with our pack of sandwiches and flask of coffee. I imagine that not many people have picnicked under cover of a motoscafi landing stage on the banks of the Canal Grande before dawn. Come to think of it, I am in no hurry to repeat the experience, once is quite enough, it was chillingly eerie as well as chillingly cold.

At 6 o'clock things began to stir and the station buffet opened. Fortified with more steaming coffee the day began and we set off along the Lista di Spagna. Flower sellers were already setting up their stands; hotel porters were on the move trundling hefty handcarts of luggage to and fro over the uneven cobbles. The Campo Ghetto Nuovo or Jewish Quarter was close by and the grey twilight gave it a memorable melancholy, its silence and austerity poignantly impressive. In Campo Nuovo a bronze bass-relief bears witness to the mass deportation of many Ghetto inhabitants to German concentration camps in 1943 and 1944.

Subdued and somewhat thoughtful we wandered on to the Fondamento Nuove looking eastwards over a lagoon which to our consternation our map called the Laguna Morta. The island gradually appearing through the mist must then be the burial ground of Venice, San Michele, resting-place of many illustrious artists, writers, and composers including Stravinski. The theme persisted. Somewhere in the area between the Ghetto and Fondamenta Nuove in a small square known as Piazzetta Funebra, we observed a flotilla of funeral gondolas, some of which were being prepared for service. As we passed, an undertaker's porter appeared practically hidden by his burden of an enormous wreath of red and white flowers. It must have measured at least the length of the coffin. This was the reality of 'Death in Venice'. These blatant reminders of man's mortality were not at all what we had expected of the city of farniente where the sundials commend one and all to 'count only the happy hours'. And now, to cap it all, a persistent drizzle set in.

The mood improved in spite of the weather as we dodged in and out of a few of the 190 churches with their various masterpieces of art and architecture. St John and St Paul's church, Gothic, (1234 - 1430) is one that I remember well, perhaps because of its spacious interior. This is the pantheon of Venice and contains many tombs of doges and patricians. Nearby stands the great equestrian statue of Colleoni the masterpiece by Verrocchio.

By this time, the citizens of Venice were on the move, going to work, or school or to the market. All was bustle beneath a moving canopy of umbrellas and we felt very much a part of it. St Mark's Square seemed a million miles away with its milling crowds of tourists and somehow or other we managed to avoid being drawn into that crowd throughout the entire day, though we did come close on the way to the Arsenal by way of Riva Schiavoni. Piazza San Marco heaved with humanity while the Arsenale was a haven of peace and tranquilly.

At some point on our wanderings our attention was caught by a poster announcing an organ recital to be given that very evening by one of the world's most eminent recitalists, Marie Claire Alain. A note was made of time and venue and the resolve made to be there. This was a rare opportunity not to be missed.

Most of the afternoon was spent relaxing over a leisurely meal; the time to dry off and rest was relished and lingered over. In contrast to the earlier melancholy mood we were here entertained by the arrival of a wedding party, the bridal pair making their way to the restaurant on foot protected only by the ubiquitous umbrella.

The crowning moment of a momentous day came with the evening recital. The concert hall of the Conservatorio di

Musica Benedetto Marcello was a perfect setting, lit by glorious chandeliers the pillared classical hall had a fine new organ built by Franz Zanin in 1986. Marie Claire Alain's programme was entirely comprised of works by her late brother, Jehan Alain, who was killed in action in 1940 at the age of 29. She introduced the music herself from the floor of the salon before taking her place at the console, which can be rather remote from the audience. The intimacy and directness added a lot to the whole experience; it was one that would never be forgotten.

At midnight, we returned to the station absolutely dropping with tiredness but content with the multifarious aspects of the day as we climbed aboard the train. With the luxury of a first class ticket we had a compartment to ourselves and slept for the entire journey almost overshooting our destined stop. When we left the train at 4:30am it was raining, it was cold too but the intimation that summer was dying indicated that the time had come to move on.

Two days later, on the 13th of October we made the ascent of our marble steps for the last time, laboriously dragging our belongings up to the car. It took two climbs to complete the loading before we could finally bid goodbye to the 'stairway of roses' and begin the journey to the south of Spain. It took 5 days to cover the 1,300 miles to the Andalusian town of Almunecar where it was to be hoped that we could spend the winter. The only way, at least the only direct way to the south was by the coast road and at the time this was very hard work. Traffic was heavy becoming increasingly congested as each of the many towns on the route had to be negotiated. Sometimes motorways were the only sensible solution, we just had to come to terms with paying the tolls, but from Alicante onwards there were no motorways, no alternative but to join the long convoy of slow moving commercial traffic heading for Murcia. Things became easier as we crossed the wild and desolate desert dunes, one of Spain's most arid inhospitable regions yet paradoxically its austerity was serenely beautiful.

The arrival in Almunecar was something of an anticlimax. The ability to track down the ideal pied-à-terre within hours of arrival seemed to have deserted us and we were forced to mark time over a weekend courtesy of a modest Hostal. On Monday morning after drawing several blanks, and more out of curiosity than hope, we walked past the villa where we had received hospitality from the Marples two years earlier. It was unoccupied. We decided to try to locate the agent, - we had been introduced by Philip but had only vague memories of the address - and the upshot was we found him and after brief negotiations the villa was ours, initially for 3 months with a possibility of extending.

It was in a state of disbelief tempered by euphoric relief that we took possession. A whole house to ourselves, 2 bedrooms, 2 bathrooms, large lounge, dining room, fitted kitchen (albeit inhabited by woodworm) a games room and best of all, a good sized swimming pool in a green secluded garden. All this for a mere 40,000pts. (£200) per month. We felt we had struck gold. Carlos Gonzalez Velasco, our agent, called two days later to collect the first month's rent and far from seeming like a business deal it was the first of many social calls. Carlos spoke excellent English, he was in fact married to an English woman called Marnie whom we were soon to meet and subsequently became good friends. Many a problem was ironed out with their assistance besides being a great source of useful information that added greatly to the quality of our time there. The thought occurred to us that had in not been for that chance meeting with Philip Marples we would not now be so comfortably situated. We wondered about them, had they been back? and the answer apparently was no, Carlos and Marnie had had no word from them since the winter of our brief convergence.

I must now set the scene of what was to become a second home over the following five or six years. The house was situated in a quiet residential area that wound its way haphazardly uphill between the promenade and the N340 the main arterial coast road. The villas came in all shapes and sizes with, for the most part, brilliantly colourful gardens, but some jealously hid their gardens behind forbiddingly high stone walls. Few of the houses had numbers or names including ours (English owned but for some reason never given identity) which made us wonder how the mail ever reached the correct address. It was quite sometime before we even discovered the name of our road, Baranco de la Cruz, but meanwhile, for our own convenience, we decided that Casa Anonyma would be a suitably apt label. However to be on the safe side Carlos suggested that we use his address for mail, and he never seemed to find it onerous to call on his way into town in his self appointed role of postman. Talking, even in a foreign language, was a favourite activity of our new friend and between us we solved many of the world's great problems.

Over the ensuing weeks, the pattern was set for our new way of life. Walking as always, was a favourite occupation, a daily swim in our own pool was a much valued luxury, even domestic chores, pottering in the garden and shopping for food had a certain aura of glamour in such surroundings. Food shopping in a recently built Moorish style market hall was always a particular pleasure especially in the fish department, and the overwhelming heaps of fruit and vegetables at unbelievably economical prices. We also discovered another new amenity in the town; a concert hall also built in the Moorish style, the Casa della Cultura. We learned through Marnie of the existence of a thriving music club that brought in many reputable soloists and chamber groups and these took place every other week. These quickly became a regular feature of our calendar adding greatly to the hedonistic lifestyle.

I had kept a diary from the outset of our travels in '82 and with the aid of a newly acquired portable typewriter I began to attempt to make a narrative account of what were in some cases mere cryptic notes. The aim was to set aside a short period of time each day for this pursuit but as with many a good resolution, it didn't always work out. The temptation to slack was great, the diversions manifold, not least of which were the amazing number of instant friendships that occurred. Sometimes these might be of short duration but highly concentrated as in the case of a casual exchange of greetings at a news stand with a Leeds couple on holiday that led to almost daily meetings. Ernest and Marie Farnhill became close friends for a week. Life histories were exchanged revealing many shared interests and they even went to the trouble of collecting a carload of driftwood for our open fire because, on two evenings they had shared the pleasure of a fireside with us. Although daytime temperatures were still warm enough to eat out of doors and even to enjoy a short dip in the pool, after sunset it became decidedly chilly. This was early December after all.

These intense social exchanges were rather like many a holiday romance in that the intention was to keep them up, whereas paths rarely crossed again. On the other hand there were friendships that prospered and despite national barriers have in fact grown in strength in subsequent years. The first of these began with a chance encounter at a pre-Christmas concert at the Casa della Cultura. Sitting in adjacent seats and overhearing each others conversation led to an instant exchange with Haakon and Kirsten Rønevik, and with the establishment of the Norwegian connection we were quickly latched on to and in a way became their family substitute. As with so many nationalities from the north the Mediterranean was a tremendous magnet, especially with pensioners who came south in droves to escape the rigorous northern winters. This was fine but with Christmas in the offing Kirsten was feeling pangs of homesickness for her family. We got on well together with emotional needs fulfilled on both sides. Although well into their 70s Haakon had the demeanour of a sprightly dapper 60 odd year old, loved a joke and enjoyed telling a tale especially when aided and abetted by a convivial bottle or two. Kirsten too bubbled with fun. She had a generous nature and a figure to go with it, plump and motherly, with a lovely head of dark hair completely innocent of any trace of grey that must have been the envy of many younger women.

For three years we continued to meet on these winter escapes with many pleasant days and evenings shared but in the early 90s, Haakon suffered a fairly serious heart attack that brought an end to their journeys south. There was however a happy post-script to this relationship. In the spring of 1991 we toured Denmark, Sweden and Norway, the ultimate aim being to visit Robert and his Norwegian wife, Else Marie who now had a 10-month-old son, Erlend Magnus. But first we had the opportunity of spending a few days with Haakon and Kirsten at their home in Årnes near Oslo. A highlight of this very pleasant visit was a long postponed tour of the capitol with Haakon as our guide. We went into the city by train, walked the sights taking in the impressive Frognerpark, home to a fantastic collection of 192 sculptures by Gustav Vigeland illustrating man's journey from the cradle to the grave. Our tour ended with a visit to the National Gallery where our guide led us to one particular painting, a portrait by the prolific artist, Edvard Munch of a rather dissipated looking young man aptly titled The Rake. And the 'rake' was actually an uncle of Haakon's, his father's brother, who had died of over indulgence at the early age of 25. A snapshot of uncle and nephew made an excellent framed enlargement which we sent subsequently to mark Haakon's 80th birthday. Christmas cards were exchanged over the next few years and then sadly came silence, an inevitable conclusion to more than one of these associations of the 'third age'.

There were several expatriates from our own country with whom we became intimates and through whom we made other fascinating contacts of various nationalities. There were two couples in particular who played an important part in our social wellbeing and these too are now depleted, having each lost a partner. We still visit Barbara, widow of Reggie Simpson, in her 10th floor flat with its panoramic sea view and amazing miniature garden on a balcony. Her family in England have not been able to entice her to return to the fold, she preferring her independence in the salubrious climate of the south, and a circle of good friends and wide interests. As well as gardens Barbara's talents run to needlework and painting, sometimes in combination, and now in her upper 70's she makes an arduous drive one day each week into the mountains for a painting session where she shares a model with a friend for Life portraits.

Through Barbara and Reggie we met George and Kay, the latter also being a keen amateur artist plus the facility to play the part of hostess. She seemed to have an uncanny knack of bringing people of various types and nationalities together. At Christmas 1989 these two septuagenarians organised a three nations party to which we were invited, where we met Peter and Chris Nissen from Denmark and Ingrid and Ulf Grundel from Sweden. These friendships developed and were further enhanced when they too offered us hospitality during the spring tour of Scandinavia. In each case their command of our language puts us to shame and all we can do to reciprocate is to show as much interest in the affairs of their respective countries as possible.

In addition to these new social exchanges, family and friends, curious to discover what kept us from hearth and home for such extended periods, came down to investigate. The first of these, and a welcome novelty for us, were my brother and sister in law, Frank and Jennifer and their son Richard who came for two weeks in March 1988, for what proved to be a successful holiday for us all. We enjoyed playing at being tour guides seeing what had by this time become familiar through the fresh consciousness of newcomers. This aspect began to pall when repeated over and over again with later visitors but we were always glad to have the social contact and exchange of news and views.

Ten days after the departure of Frank and Jennifer, our second son and his wife, Edmund and Sue, arrived in the evening of April 7th. We met them at the airport at Malaga, a joyful meeting especially for us as this was the first time in the six years since the travel project was set in motion that we had the chance to share a little of our doctrine of hedonism with a son. It was difficult not to feel a twinge or two of guilt when our offspring were caught up in the 'mortal coil' and I had to remind myself that we had been through this stage ourselves and could well have to face up to more in the future. Meanwhile this period was as close to our golden age as we were ever likely to reach again.

Between these two visits Easter occurred, our first in the deep south and despite having seen many pictures of the ceremonial religious processions, the reality made quite a deep impression. Our introduction came on the Tuesday of Semana Santa, Holy Week, when a procession was due to commence at 9:0 pm from the church. In fact half an hour of what seemed to us chaotic disorganisation passed before a miraculous order was restored and the procession of hooded penitents accompanied by the tattoo of drum and trumpet bands got under way. Then came the first of many pasos borne aloft by groups of men known as costaleros. Each paso represented a stage in the final week of the life of Christ, life-size effigies decorated with hundreds of flowers and coloured lights and though many might be bordering on gaudiness they still had a compelling power. The aspect that I found most deeply moving was the discipline of the bearers. Swaying gently in complete harmony and dignity, they moved as one, as though impelled by a single motivating force. And they kept up this slow and steady pace for hours with pauses at intervals to relieve the weight from their shoulders. One night, Thursday I believe it was, we counted five of these pasos and at least as many groups of musicians, not to mention endless lines of hooded penitents, many of them children, all in groups, with each group clad in different coloured robes. The processions could go on for several hours finishing perhaps at three or even four in the morning. We were not sure if this was from devotion to their faith or for love of theatricality and dressing up. Either way they certainly required dedication and endurance.

With the departure of Edmund and Sue the moment came for our exodus. It was time to fly north with the swallows and once again there was no doubt in our minds that the lure of the south would bring us back sooner or later. For economic reasons it was not until November '89 that we returned. This time we made the journey easier by crossing from Plymouth to Santander aboard the fine new ship, The Bretagne, launched only the previous July. Being the off season there were comparatively few passengers and we received 5 star treatment, a beautiful cabin, spacious and with a full observation window for the price of a basic one deep down in the bowels of the ship. The public rooms too were luxurious, shared only with a handful of other passengers. It was quite the best beginning one could imagine, 24 hours of relaxing travel in absolute comfort. The chance of a repeat of such a fortuitous experience is now remote with the increase in numbers of people on the move.

The 2 day journey across the Peninsula came as a revelation; infinitely more exciting than the coastal route and the first of many journeys that we made subsequently through practically every region of Spain. This time we took a fairly direct road south. Lovely green mountains topped by rugged crags above which, at frequent intervals soared great birds of prey that we took to be eagles but later discovered were griffin vultures. Such was the topography of the early stages of the day. Then came the cities, Segovia the graceful city on a hill looking like a picture from a Gothic fairytale, and Avila with its incredible turreted crenellated walls that are so complete. Here we found a room for the night in a hotel backing onto the wall and adjacent to the Rastro Gate, a wonderfully atmospheric place. As always in inland Spain, dinner was not until 9 o'clock which meant a wait of two hours, but a huge log fire in a cavern of a hall plus a bottle of wine, a loaf of bread and some olives filled the gap in more ways than one.

The next day we crossed the Sierra de Gredos from where we had a birds-eye view of the Escorial Palace, a gloomy place by all accounts but quite magical from this perspective. On through Toledo another remarkably situated city, on a bluff that is dominated by the ruins of the Alcazar, then came the unusual windmills of Consuegra with its associations with the famous Don Quixote. The remainder of that journey was a series of frustrations, long hold ups for road works, torrential downpours, and a long slow crawl negotiating Granada's rush hour. It was dark when we reached Casa

Anonyma, but the air was warm and sweet smelling, filled with the song of cicadas. It was wonderful to be back.

And so the threads were taken up once again, the mixture not quite as before the basic ingredients were there but spiced with seemingly illimitable variations. One extra dimension on this trip was the addition of our bicycles that had travelled safely for 4 days on a roof rack. This gave greater mobility and scope for exploring further afield without constant use of the car. However the terrain was not all plain sailing, there was quite a bit of pushing to be done on the steep hill sections. Looking back, that winter seems to have been one long social whirl interspersed by great discoveries of countryside fauna and flora. The revels began as already described, at Christmas with the cosmopolitan lunch party and this was followed by a combined Birthday cum New Year party given by George and Kay in their own apartment. Here were gathered the greatest number of ex-patriots we had yet encountered, 15 in all, many of whom lived permanently on the Costa del Sol while a few like ourselves were simply winter migrants.

At the end of January Eric and I celebrated our 36th wedding anniversary with our own international luncheon party; the Norwegians, Swedes, and Danes along with the English, represented by Barbara and Reggie. Unfortunately, Kay and George were unable to join us through indisposition. A unique aspect of this party was being able to dine al fresco in mid-winter, a feature of life in the south that has always been a great pleasure to us.

February was almost entirely taken up by visits from friends, Dave and Vivian from Heswall at the beginning of the month with Lin and Gill arriving just 5 days later. These were good times but consecutive visits did require constant exertion and extra effort so a short period of calm was necessary to regain ones equilibrium. By mid-March fully rested we were ready to celebrate my 60th birthday by visiting Madrid. We decided to leave the car at home and let a bus do the work, it was a ten hour journey with a break mid-way for lunch, and thus from the comfort of our elevated seats, busses being so much higher than cars, we could view the passing scene and ignore the traffic. We spent two nights at the Hotel Carlton, 4 stars and rather grand but it was a special occasion. We found an excellent Chinese restaurant serving meals at the early hour of 8 o'clock so decided to relinquish our usual 'when in Rome' policy and take advantage of a meal at a civilised hour. It was a good decision, fine food good wine and a complimentary saki to finish. The following day we walked the sights, and walked and walked, we must have covered teens of miles, and yet in the evening we still had enough energy left to hop on the metro and search out the Auditorio Nacional di Musica where the choir and orchestra National de Espana were to perform Beethoven's Missa Solemnis. The conductor and soloists were English, the former being Walter Weller but of particular interest to us was the soprano soloist Lynda Russell who had been a fellow student of Robert at the Royal College of music and had sung at his wedding. The concert hall was magnificent. It was very new, light, well proportioned and our seats alongside the orchestra gave us ideal vision and sound. It was the high spot of an extra special day. On the way back to the city centre, as we walked past a church, to our surprise a wedding party emerged in all their glory and this was about 10:30 at night. We dined again at 'our' Chinese restaurant passing the house where Cervantes had lived and finally collapsed into bed well after midnight. My 60th birthday had been an unforgettable day, the only fly in the ointment being a frustrated wish to visit the Prado Museum of art. Our visit happened to coincide with a special exhibition of the works of Velasquez. Good was our initial reaction, that is until we saw the queue, which must have stretched for almost a quarter of a mile and moved forward at a snail's pace. Had we joined that shuffling line it would have taken hours, and with only one day at our disposal it was impossible to contemplate. A far more disconcerting blemish occurred during the bus journey home on the third day, a Sunday. All was well to begin with, quiet roads meant we made good time, and the driver's choice of background music, instead of the usual local radio trivialities, was a tape of tenor arias. After the mid-morning coffee break, the driver decided it was time for the inevitable video and that is when the rot set in. It was a violent American film of gang rape, murder and revenge from which the captive audience of predominantly older people could not escape. You could try to avoid it by looking out of the windows but there was no ignoring the soundtrack. Two hours of this ghastly film ruined the journey, the atmosphere remaining long after the end of the film making a mockery of any attempt to enjoy the passing scene. Incidentally, a polite request that the sound might be reduced seemed to fall on deaf ears; it was apparently assumed that all the passengers were enthusiastic over the choice of entertainment.

Towards the end of April and our allotted residence in Almunecar a proposed visit by our third son Richard and three grandchildren was aborted due to failure to procure flights to Malaga but instead they were able to get seats to Faro and asked us to join them there. This we did and thus had our first look at Portugal. The Algarve coast was attractive with many appealing sandy coves and beaches which was fine for entertaining the children but our general impression of the countryside was that it lacked the grandeur that we had become accustomed to in Andalusia.

We saw the family off at Faro on the 29th and set off ourselves on the return journey north, first re-crossing the Guadiano by a rickety old ferry into Spain. This ferry has now been replaced by a magnificent and graceful suspension bridge. Our route from here was completely new: Seville, Cordoba, Bailen, stopping overnight at an inexpensive hostal at La Carolina. The Spanish hostal system suited our purposes admirably being almost unfailingly well appointed, adequate and cheap. Being the ad hoc travellers that we were - and still are for that matter - we never booked ahead and only once failed to find good shelter, be it for one night or longer as the need determined. For the next three days we made our way cross-country taking in such places as El Toboso in the heart of Don Quixote territory with its windmills galore, Cuenca with its incredible houses that hang over precipitous cliffs, through ever changing scenery of many coloured rock and earth, tableland and mountain, forest and prairie. At Ejea de Caballeros storks seemed to be nesting on every rooftop and later still, as we approached the Pyrenees, there were great numbers of black and red kites. At the night stop we found we had the mountain hostal to ourselves. A spotlessly clean and comfortable room with a fantastic mountain and lake view was ours for the princely sum of £10.

The blueprint was now set for future journeys, the next being a three month period, March to May in 1991 when we stayed again in Almunecar and this was followed later the same year by six weeks on the move covering in depth places previously only glimpsed in passing. The outstanding excursion of this autumn trip was a four-hour safari aboard dune buggies over the immense sand dunes of the Cota Donana National Park. Being the dry season we missed out on the flamingos and other water birds for which the area is famed, but the bush life of wild cattle, horses, deer, and boar were plentiful and there was no shortage of magnificent birds of prey. We have since heard that this wonderful wilderness is threatened by developers, a golfing resort having been mooted amongst other equally outrageous possibilities. We just hope that sense will prevail and conservationists will win the day.

Another wild area, (not so far as we know under threat) we found in Las Alpujarras, that mountain region southeast of Granada. Communities remain almost untouched in their isolation from the main steam of our own times and if the writer Gerald Brenan could be reincarnated and visit Yegen, the village where he lived and wrote in the '20s', he would surely find that little had changed. The area is a veritable wonderland for anyone interested in botany, ornithology etc. In winter the mountain slopes from the snowline down are a symphony of pink, the blossom of the almond trees, a principle crop of these harsh upper slopes. Wild stocks scent the air and the roadsides everywhere are a kaleidoscope of brightly coloured alpine flowers. Hoopoes might take flight round a bend in the road, alarm crest erect, a magnificent sight, whilst in a sheltered orchard Bee-eaters frolic like a living rainbow. It is not easy driving, the road twists and turns constantly, it took us five hours to drive from Almeria to Motril which by the coast road would take only two hours, but the rewards are many and varied.

The last five years have seen a change in family commitments that has restricted freedom for extended travel, wings have been somewhat clipped but not totally. Meanwhile we mark time and compromise. Home is now an interesting converted chapel in the gentle hills of mid-Wales, a far cry from Spanish sierras it may be but it has a fascination of its own and gives endless scope for the insatiable urge to explore fresh territory. A remarkable network of quiet lanes river valleys, wooded hills and fine estuaries offer endless variety for walking, while another batch of new acquaintances satisfies social needs. Our experience of changes of environment seems to give the lie to the general opinion that retirement is not a sensible time for moving. I have no doubt that this is good advice for some but other's, like us, appear to thrive on fresh stimulus and one day when the present restraint is relaxed, whether we are in our 70's or beyond, if health and strength is still ours. Shangri la in the shape of Casa Anonyma is there, waiting for our return. The will is still strong to follow our inclination and answer the call of the south.

Patricia Coates was born in Manchester in 1930, and educated at Levenshulme Grammar school. She married in 1954, and had four sons.

An early urrge to travel first manifested itself in numerous house moves; from Cheadle in Cheshire the family moved first to Preston and from there to the Isle of Man.

Travels abroad began with a train journey to Italy in the mid 70's, followed by driving holidays in France and Italy. Notes kept at this time grew into articles, some of which appeared in Manx Life magazine.

The Author now lives in Powys – Mid Wales.